EMULATION-WORKI
EXPLAINED

A Practical Handbook for the Guidance of Officers, from the Master to the Outer Guard, in Craft Lodges under the jurisdiction of the United Grand Lodge of England

BY

HERBERT F. INMAN, L.R.

P.M. Gihon Lodge, 49; P.M. & D.C. Horus Lodge, 3155
P.M. Lodge of the Men of Kent and Kentish
Men, 4273; Mid-Kent Masters' Lodge, 3173;
Hon. Member Ad Astra Lodge, 3808;
P.Z. & Scribe E. Crays Valley
Chapter, 2147; P.Z. Horus
Chapter, 3155.

———

Member of the Committee of the Emulation Lodge of
Improvement, January 1926–March 1929.

———

Preceptor Horus Lodge of Instruction.

———

Preceptor Ad Astra L.I. 1920–1924
Deputy Preceptor Peter Gilkes L.I. 1917–1925
Deputy Preceptor St Bride L.I. 1918–1920

(Third Edition)

A. LEWIS, 13 PATERNOSTER ROW, E.C.
1935

Kessinger Publishing's Rare Reprints
Thousands of Scarce and Hard-to-Find Books!

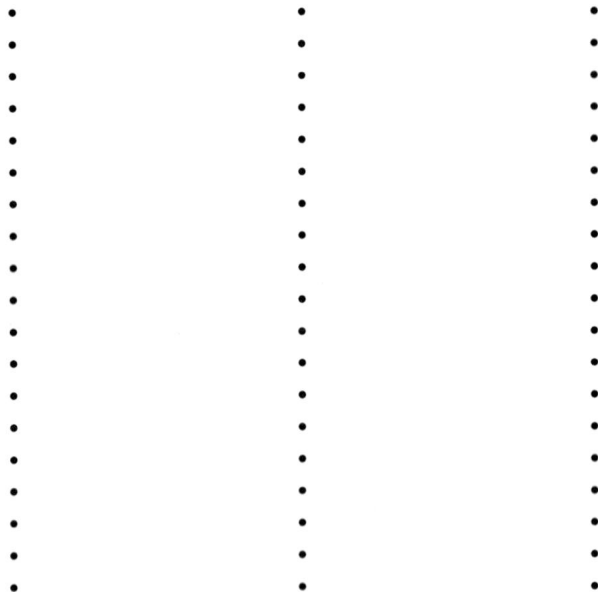

First published in November 1929
Second and revised edition, September 1932
Third   „   „   „   August 1935

Printed in Great Britain

DEDICATED BY KIND PERMISSION

TO

The Right Honourable
The LORD CORNWALLIS, C.B.E.,

DEPUTY GRAND MASTER

OF THE UNITED GRAND LODGE OF ENGLAND

AND

PROVINCIAL GRAND MASTER

OF KENT

"Then I realised for the first time what word-and-gesture-perfect ritual could be brought to mean."

RUDYARD KIPLING,
In the Interests of the Brethren.

CONTENTS

CHAPTER   PAGE

DEDICATION 5
FOREWORD 11
AUTHOR'S PREFACE TO THE FIRST EDITION 13
AUTHOR'S PREFACE TO THE SECOND EDITION 19

PART I

(Some Facts about Emulation)

I. WHAT IS EMULATION ? 23
II. EMULATION AND THE GRAND STEWARDS . 37
III. THE EMULATION LECTURES . . . 53
IV. THE EMULATION MATCH-BOX . . 60
V. THE EMULATION COMMITTEE . . . 65
VI. SQUARING THE LODGE 73
VII. SOME DIFFERENCES OF WORKING . . 76

PART II

(The Officers of the Lodge and their Duties)

THE OFFICERS OF THE LODGE . . 85
VIII. THE TYLER 87
IX. THE STEWARD 93
X. THE INNER GUARD 96
XI. THE ASSISTANT SECRETARY . . . 111

CHAPTER		PAGE
XII.	The Organist	114
XIII.	The Almoner	117
XIV.	The Assistant Director of Cere-monies	120
XV.	The Deacons	123
XVI.	The Junior Deacon . . .	130
XVII.	The Senior Deacon . . .	142
XVIII.	The Director of Ceremonies . .	155
XIX.	The Secretary	176
XX.	The Treasurer	184
XXI.	The Chaplain	187
XXII.	The Wardens	191
XXIII.	The Junior Warden . . .	198
XXIV.	The Senior Warden . . .	204
XXV.	The Immediate Past Master . .	211
XXVI.	The Worshipful Master . .	217
XXVII.	The Worshipful Master (contd.) .	233

PART III

(*Miscellaneous Matters*)

XXVIII.	The Lodge of Instruction . .	255
XXIX.	Smoking at Refreshment . .	269
XXX.	Masonic Don'ts	275
	Appendix A (List of Recognised Lodges of Instruction)	283
	Appendix B (Table of Knocks) . .	285
	Appendix C (Letter from V.W. Bro. Sir Edward Letchworth, G.S.) .	287
	General Index	289

FOREWORD

By W. Bro. The Rev. JOSEPH JOHNSON, P.A.G. Chaplain.

IT is with very real pleasure that I write a foreword to this book. The author, W. Bro. Herbert F. Inman, L.R., has been known to me in Masonic circles for a number of years, and a more earnest and capable Brother I have not met. From the commencement of his Masonic career he has been eager to acquire knowledge of Freemasonry and has earnestly studied differing Rituals, with the result that he is a convinced adherent to Emulation and is acknowledged as a most capable exponent.

This book is a Manual of Instruction and Guidance for Masons, and is written *by* a worker *for* workers in strict accordance with the recognised system of the Emulation Lodge of Improvement. The supreme motive of Bro. Inman in writing this book has been to stimulate Brethren to become proficient in working the different Ceremonies of the Craft. Like all who take Masonry seriously, he has a great abhorrence of inefficiency and slovenliness in working the Craft ritual. He advocates that in the working of Lodge Ceremonies there shall be complete mastery of the Ritual, with accuracy in every detail of procedure.

The author knows from long experience the deplorable ignorance of correct procedure which is often manifested, and how many Brethren suffer through lack of competent tuition. The result is that Candidates are not impressed with the Lodge Ceremonies as they should be, and as they would be if the Ceremonies were carried through with ease and dignity.

This book provides ample explanation and reliable guidance for all Brethren who desire adequate equipment for their duties, whatever their nature or degree. The author has had long experience as a Preceptor of several Lodges of Instruction, and is recognised as an expert Instructor in Emulation-working.

I have read the proofs of this book with intense pleasure and unhesitatingly commend it to my Brethren who, in this and other lands, are wishful for trustworthy guidance in their effort to acquire efficiency in the work of Craft Lodges.

J. J.

EMULATION-WORKING EXPLAINED

AUTHOR'S PREFACE TO THE FIRST EDITION

" The Master-Elect has offered me a collar ; I must begin to look up the work."

How often we hear some similar remark from the young Mason who is soon to place his foot upon one of the lower rungs of the ladder of Masonic progress! He is about to be entrusted with a position of the utmost importance and responsibility—for all Masonic Offices may be so described—and he therefore decides that it is high time he *began* to seek that knowledge which he should long since have acquired.

It is not difficult to imagine the disastrous consequences which would certainly ensue in the outer world of business life for the man who deferred preparation for the responsibilities of a higher post in the sphere of his particular daily avocation until *after* his preferment. Yet, in Masonry, procrastination and indifference are all too frequently in evidence.

In the Fourth of the Antient Charges we are told: "*All preferment among Masons is grounded upon real worth and personal merit only. . . . Therefore no Master or Warden is chosen by seniority, but for his merit.*"

An admirable counsel of perfection, but one which, it is to be feared, has for many years been honoured more in the breach than in the observance. All too common has become the practice of promoting Brethren according to their position in the Lodge list of Members, with little or no thought as to their qualifications, or as to the manner in which they are likely to discharge the duties appertaining to their Office.

Senior Past Masters cannot be held entirely free from censure in this connection, for there must be many who read these words who have known the youthful and zealous Master-Elect who, desirous of appointing as his Officers the most capable of his Brethren, has allowed himself to be influenced by the solemn warnings of his seniors against "causing a split in the Lodge," "disturbing the harmony," and so on *ad infinitum*.

Harmony and Fraternity, of course, must not be lightly disturbed, but the impressive dignity and solemn beauty of our Ceremonies and Rites are of equal importance, and these desirable effects are to be obtained only when the Master and his Officers are efficient in every detail of their manifold responsibilities.

A Lodge of Freemasons is "an assemblage of Brethren met to expatiate on the mysteries of the Craft," as we are reminded in the opening Section of the First Lecture. Let the framework of that Lodge be insecure in any of its parts and the entire structure must suffer, with consequent confusion and undignified blundering during those grave proceedings which should at all times be characterised by ennobling dignity, awe-inspiring solemnity, and perfect smoothness of execution.

"*All preferment among Masons is grounded upon real worth and personal merit only.*"

Much remains to be done before this counsel of perfection becomes the universal rule. But much has already been done, and there are to-day welcome indications that Masters-Elect and Lodge Committees *are* paying more careful consideration to the qualifications of prospective Officers. Also, with the continued and rapid growth in the number of reliable Lodges of Instruction, there is to be found among the younger members of the Fraternity a healthy spirit of inquiry and a desire for knowledge, combined with an increasing and laudable determination to become proficient in their various duties.

It would scarcely be possible to pay too high a tribute to the valuable work done in our Lodges of Instruction*; but, with it all, Preceptors are busy

* See p. 283 for list of recognised Emulation-working Lodges of Instruction.

men, and the time at their disposal at the weekly meetings is usually limited to about an hour and a half.   Therefore it may well happen that even the diligent young Mason who attends his Lodge of Instruction with fair regularity may still be left in doubt on many points in connection with his duties, quite apart from the words and phrases which he seeks to memorise within the peaceful seclusion of his abiding-place.

It is for such of our younger Brethren that this little Manual has been compiled, in the earnest hope that they may find it of some practical assistance. It has been written in no dictatorial spirit, but with one desire only, to aid the newly invested Officer in his search for that knowledge with which he must be armed if he is to reflect honour on the choice of the Worshipful Brother who has given him his preferment.   It is to be hoped that the suggestions and guiding hints contained herein will be accepted in the same fraternal spirit in which they are freely offered.   The author certainly has no desire arrogantly to assume that, because he believes a certain method to be desirable, therefore all others must of necessity be wrong.

In all save essentials our Craft Ceremonies vary considerably in the many different systems of Ritual now to be witnessed during one's Masonic travels, and it will readily be understood that, within the scope of so small a work, it has been found advisable to limit specific directions to one popular and well-known form of working. The author, having served a lengthy period of apprenticeship as Preceptor in various Lodges of Instruction working under the official ægis of the Emulation Lodge of Improvement, prior to his election to the governing body of that famous School of Masonic Ritual, may perhaps lay humble claim to speak with some authority in relation thereto.

It is to be understood, therefore, that in all cases where definite directions are given with regard to the duties of any Officer *within the Lodge* the *Emulation system* is referred to. Such directions may be relied upon as being accurate in every detail, although, be it noted, they are given solely on the author's personal authority, and are in no sense to be accepted as official pronouncements from the Committee of Emulation Lodge of Improvement. Emulation Lodge of Improvement is governed to-day, as it has always been governed during the hundred odd years of its existence, by a Committee of expert Past Masters; any authoritative ruling from that Committee is only to be obtained through the Secretary, *in his official capacity as such.*

The amount of labour involved in the preparation of this Handbook has been greater than may be apparent at a casual glance. Limitations of space demanded drastic restrictions, and not the least difficult part of the task has been to judge that which should be omitted rather than that which should be written. This Manual, of course, is not intended in

2

any sense to take the place of the printed Ritual; it should be read in conjunction with that Ritual.*

In the hope that his efforts have not been altogether unsuccessful, the author now offers them with his fraternal greetings to his Brethren in the Ancient and Honourable Institution which rests upon the sure foundation of the practice of every Moral and Social Virtue.   H. F. I.

November, 1929.

---

* No printed version of the Ceremonies or Lectures has ever received the official sanction or approval of the Committee of the Emulation Lodge of Improvement. Nevertheless the indisputable fact remains that the workers at Emulation and at the recognised Lodges of Instruction owe their proficiency very largely to the printed ritual. To learn the Ceremonies merely by listening to them would obviously take many years, and few Brethren would ever attain to anything approaching that standard of word-accuracy which distinguishes the work of the majority of keen Emulation-workers.

Without for a moment questioning the wisdom of the attitude adopted by the Emulation Committee towards printed books of ritual, yet the existence and usefulness of such rituals cannot be ignored. Any claim that the Emulation Ceremonies are learnt independently of the assistance of the printed ritual will not bear the test of examination. One particular ritual has been used in the past, and is used to-day, by practically all the Preceptors of the recognised Lodges of Instruction, and these learned Brethren wisely recommend it to their pupils. This same ritual, which was first issued more than seventy years ago, has been of incalculable benefit to many thousands of Emulation-workers in all parts of the world.

The ritual referred to is *The Perfect Ceremonies of Craft Masonry* (published by Messrs A. Lewis, 13 Paternoster Row, London, E.C.4), recently revised under the personal supervision of the Preceptor of one of the leading recognised Lodges of Instruction. The present writer unhesitatingly recommends this ritual to all students desirous of attaining perfection in the Emulation Ceremonies.—H. F. I.

AUTHOR'S PREFACE TO THE SECOND EDITION

IN introducing the Second Edition of this Manual the author's first duty is a happy one—to express sincere thanks to his Brethren, not only in London and the Provinces, but also in several of the distant Districts over the seas, for the many fraternal and encouraging congratulations he has received in communications expressing appreciation of the First Edition.

Many correspondents have been good enough to offer suggestions for additional matter for incorporation in future editions. Limitations of space alone preclude the adoption of more than a small number of these welcome suggestions.

There has been a widespread desire for more detailed information relating to matters connected with the Emulation Lodge of Improvement (apart from the actual Ritual and Ceremonial) and perhaps the additional chapters now included in Part I of the Second Edition will meet this request.

In Part II the detailed instructions tendered for the guidance of Lodge Officers have been amplified in many directions, and the author offers this

Second Edition of the Manual to his Brethren in
the hope that it may meet with a reception at least
as gratifying as that accorded to the First Edition.

H. F. I.

September 1932.

PART I
SOME FACTS ABOUT EMULATION

PART I
SOME FACTS ABOUT EMULATION

CHAPTER I

WHAT IS EMULATION?

To the experienced Emulation enthusiast who spends, perhaps, two or three evenings a week in a recognised Lodge of Instruction, and who rarely misses a meeting of the Emulation Lodge of Improvement at Freemasons' Hall, the query at the head of this chapter will, no doubt, appear superfluous. Those zealous and industrious ritualists, however, must remember that there are very many Brethren who have never entered the famous Lodge of Improvement, Brethren who—even though they may claim to be Emulation-workers—possess no more intimate knowledge of Emulation than is to be derived from a study of the printed ritual under the supervision of a Preceptor who, in many cases, may be as uninformed on the subject as the pupils who look to him for tuition.

For the information of such Brethren an attempt will be made to answer the query which heads this chapter. The answer must of necessity be brief, the primary object of this Manual being to provide practical hints for those Brethren who seek to perfect themselves in the Emulation Ceremonies, rather than to offer anything in the nature of a critical survey of the history of the Emulation Lodge of Improvement.

It cannot be gainsaid that the youthful Masonic student, eager for knowledge, is frequently bewildered by the multiplicity of Masonic rituals which are brought to his notice. He hears about 'Logic,' 'West End,' 'Oxford,' 'Bristol,' 'Universal,' 'North London,' and many other so-called Masonic 'workings.' No doubt he wonders what they all mean—why there are so many—whence they came. Possibly, too, being unlearned in the history of Masonic ritual, he mentally brackets Emulation with the rest, regarding it as no more than a fanciful name created by some imaginative Brother in search of a novelty.

Very briefly, it may be explained that 'Emulation'—the bare word itself—is an abbreviated form of describing the Emulation Lodge of Improvement for Master Masons, meeting at Freemasons' Hall, Great Queen Street, London, W.C.2, on Friday evenings at six o'clock, and that it is also the word used to describe the particular system of ritual taught therein.

The Lodge of Improvement was founded in 1823, its object being to teach the precise form of ritual settled by the Lodge of Reconciliation, as approved, sanctioned, and confirmed by the United Grand

Lodge of England on 5th June 1816, which sanction was duly recorded in the Minutes of Grand Lodge for that date.* The basic principle of Emulation is that none has the right to alter that ritual in word or action until such time—if ever—as the Grand Lodge may officially sanction such alteration. The claim repeatedly advanced by many eminent supporters of the famous Lodge of Improvement is that Emulation teaches to-day—and has always taught—that particular, *authorised ritual* without variation.

How far can such a claim be substantiated to-day? Any answer to this query demands some reference to the condition of affairs existing in English Craft Masonry during the early part of the nineteenth century, but such reference must necessarily be brief when the subject has to be disposed of within the scope of a single chapter.† Suffice it to say that prior to the year 1813 there existed two Grand Lodges,—one established in 1717, afterwards known as the Moderns; and the other founded in 1751, generally referred to as the Ancients. For more than sixty years bitter rivalry existed between the two bodies, but in 1813 a Union was happily consummated. Hence the present title of the *United* Grand Lodge of England. These facts are, of course, familiar to all experienced students, but we are here writing for the novice.

* See Appendix C, p. 287.
† Brethren desirous of more complete information will find many interesting details in Sadler's *History of the Emulation Lodge of Improvement.*

It is readily to be understood that the long-standing rivalry was not terminated without considerable difficulty; new regulations were essential for the government of the Craft, and the settlement of the form of ritual to be used under the newly formed Grand Lodge was, quite naturally, one of the controversial questions which gave rise to much discussion and difference of opinion.

The Articles of Union, ratified, confirmed, and sealed on 1st December 1813, stipulated that there should henceforth be *perfect unity* of working. For the purpose of establishing such unity of working the Articles further provided for the constitution of a Lodge to be styled the Lodge of Reconciliation, such Lodge to be composed of an equal number of expert Masons from each of the old Constitutions. In Article V we find that the Brethren composing the Lodge of Reconciliation were empowered to settle the form of ritual to be observed for all time.

That the Brethren of the Lodge of Reconciliation spared no efforts to arrive at unanimous and satisfactory conclusions is proved by the fact that it was not until 20th May 1816 that the Ceremonies decided upon were rehearsed before an especial meeting of the Grand Lodge, at which the M.W. the Grand Master, H.R.H. the Duke of Sussex, presided. At the next meeting of the Grand Lodge, held on 5th June 1816, the Ceremonies recommended were *approved and confirmed.*

It is seen, therefore, that in the year 1816 a particular method of opening and closing the Lodge in the Three Degrees, and of Making, Passing, and Raising Masons was approved and accepted by the United Grand Lodge on behalf of the whole of the English Fraternity. The Installation Ceremony was dealt with at a later date when, in 1827, the Grand Master, through a Board of Installed Masters, held four meetings and decided the only form of Installation Ceremony which has ever received the seal of authority.

The Lodge of Reconciliation, having fulfilled the specific purpose for which it was warranted, ceased to exist in 1816, and the propagation of the newly arranged Reconciliation Ritual devolved upon the Lodges of Instruction which came into being at that period. Of those Lodges one of the most prominent was the United Lodge of Perseverance, founded on 26th January 1818, a little more than a year after the dissolution of the Lodge of Reconciliation. This Lodge numbered amongst its members several of the most learned Masons of the day, of whom nine became Founders of the Emulation Lodge of Improvement in 1823. Others subsequently joined the Lodge of Improvement. At one of their meetings the Brethren of the United Lodge of Perseverance passed the following resolution:—

"That the Ancient Lectures and the Ceremonies of Initiating, Passing, and Raising, as confirmed by the Grand Lodge of England, be strictly adhered to in this Lodge."

The Lodge of Reconciliation, as already stated, dissolved in 1816, and the Emulation Lodge of Improvement was not founded until 1823. But this gap of seven years is reduced very considerably when it is found from reliable evidence that the Emulation Lodge of Improvement obviously emanated from the old United Lodge of Perseverance. The majority of the Brethren from the latter Lodge became enthusiastic supporters of Emulation, and it is reasonable to assume that the resolute old Masonic veterans who passed the resolution quoted above would not have permitted the slightest innovation in the working of the Reconciliation Ceremonies during their lifetime.

No review of Emulation's history, however brief, would be complete without reference to the celebrated Peter William Gilkes, a famous Masonic instructor whose name is inseparably bound up with Emulation's early activities. Writing of Peter Gilkes, the late Bro. Henry Sadler, Grand Librarian, a noted Masonic historian and author, said:

"Indeed we question whether any single individual, either before his time or since, has attained to such distinction as a Masonic instructor."

On 6th August 1818, V.W. Bro. Edwards Harper, Grand Secretary, wrote to the W.M. of Lodge 498, Shrewsbury:

"In referring you to Peter Gilkes I mentioned that he would instruct you in the *correct method* adopted since the Union."

On 6th September 1843, V.W. Bro. W. H. White, Grand Secretary, wrote to the W.M. of Lodge 523:

"Bro. Gilkes was *fully master of all the Ceremonies*, and I believe he most faithfully observed them."

Bro. Peter Gilkes was born in 1765 and died in 1833. He was Initiated in 1786 in the British Lodge, now No. 8, the Lodge which gave its sanction to the United Lodge of Perseverance, of which Lodge Gilkes was a prominent member. Peter Gilkes was present at the first meeting of the Emulation Lodge of Improvement; he became a member shortly afterwards and was Leader of the Committee in 1825.

It is worthy of note that Gilkes was an attendant at the meetings of the Lodge of Promulgation, a Lodge constituted in 1809 by the Grand Lodge of the Moderns, its object being 'the Ascertaining and Promulgating of the Ancient Landmarks of the Craft.' Put into plain words, this simply means that the members of the Lodge of Promulgation met to decide which of their own customs and practices they must insist upon when the hoped-for Union came about, and how far they would be prepared to give way to the Ancients.

A careful study of ancient Records and Minutes leads one to the conclusion that the majority of the changes which were ultimately made were decided upon in the Lodge of Promulgation between 1809 and 1811, some few years *before* the Lodge of Reconciliation was constituted. That eminent and respected Masonic historian, the late Bro. W. B. Hextall, wrote:

"The Lodge of Reconciliation adopted most of the decisions at which the Lodge of Promulgation had not long before arrived."

It is evident, therefore, that Peter Gilkes was in a position to know *beforehand* the decisions likely to be arrived at by the Lodge of Reconciliation, and that he attended that Lodge (as he did upon ten occasions) not as a pupil, but rather in the capacity of an expert critic, one who had already memorised from 'A' to 'Z' the newly arranged alphabet which others were then striving to learn. Peter Gilkes, as has been stated, became Leader of Emulation in 1825, which position he held until his death in 1833, when he was succeeded by one of his pupils, Bro. Stephen Barton Wilson.

The following is an extract from a report of the Emulation Festival held in 1835:

"The meeting was in particular marked by the presence of the three leading Lecturers on Masonry, upon whom by general consent as it were the mantle of Peter Gilkes may be said to have fallen. We feel an honest pride in our association with Bros. Dowley, Cooper, and S. B. Wilson, and entertain so high an opinion of their value to the Society that we take the liberty of making as public as we can their well-earned character for intelligence, grounded upon a careful adherence to the Landmarks of the Order, for the strict observance of our laws and regulations, and still more for the modesty with which they received the homage readily offered to their merits as individuals."

From the fact that the names of Bros. Wilson, Dowley, and Cooper are mentioned conjointly in the report as the successors to Peter Gilkes in the government of the Emulation Lodge of Improvement, it seems an obvious deduction that the Lodge was controlled then, as it is to-day, by a Committee of experienced Preceptors, selected by the members from amongst the most expert of their number.

It is this joint control by an expert Committee which is the greatest strength of the Emulation system; it affords convincing testimony as to the accuracy and reliability of Emulation's methods in the transmission of the authorised Reconciliation Ritual from those far-off days of the immediate post-Union period down to the present time. In the ordinary Lodge of Instruction as Preceptor succeeds Preceptor there is, of course, a likelihood —one might say a certainty—of innovations creeping into the work. Many of the marked differences in working now to be seen have come about within recent years, either through laxity, or as the result of the personal influence of some strong-willed and imaginative members of particular Lodges.

At the Emulation Lodge of Improvement it may fairly be claimed that anything of the sort is an impossibility, for the simple reason that there always is—and always has been—an overlapping Committee, all of one mind, all most solemnly pledged to observe and insist upon the most minute accuracy, and to prevent the slightest deviation or innovation. Seated on the left of Peter Gilkes in his day were Bros. Barton Wilson and Dowley. When Wilson succeeded Gilkes he had with him Bros. Richards and Pike, and, later, Thomas Fenn. It was Fenn who became Leader on the death of Wilson in 1866, and he was supported by Bros. Richards and Murton, and, subsequently, by Bro. Robert Clay Sudlow. Sudlow succeeded Fenn in 1883, and he had by his side for a time Bros. Spaull and Dawson. Then in succession came Bros. Rushton, Kentish, Lander, and, in 1904, the present Leader of the Committee, Bro. G. J. V. Rankin, who succeeded Sudlow as Leader in 1914. On Bro. Rankin's accession to the Leadership a fourth member was added to the Committee; he had the support of Bros. J. H. Jenks, J. J. Black, and A. Scott. Bro. Jenks retired in 1916 and was succeeded by Bro. S. Chalkley, while Bro. S. A. Knaggs took Bro. Scott's place in 1920. The rulers of Emulation are ever on the watch to safeguard the transmission of the ritual. Of recent years, the work having increased enormously, greater strain has been thrown upon the members of the Committee; therefore, at the beginning of 1926, it was decided further to enlarge the governing body. The two Brethren elected were

Bros. A. B. Wilson and Herbert F. Inman. Bro. Chalkley resigned towards the end of 1928 and was succeeded by Bro. A. J. Peyton. Bro. Inman resigned in March 1929, and was succeeded by Bro. H. C. Tasker, who was elected in January 1930.

Thus it is seen that the Emulation Committee has always been a strong, unbroken chain from the time of Peter Gilkes, and innovations, therefore, have been made as impossible as it is within the power of human nature to render them. It has to be remembered, too, that each succeeding member of the Emulation Committee has been personally instructed and drilled by his predecessor; each has to serve a lengthy period of apprenticeship, generally as the Preceptor of one of the recognised Lodges of Instruction.

Although the term 'Emulation Committee' * is generally accepted to refer to those eminent instructors who occupy the Committee Bench to take actual control of the ceremonial work at the weekly meetings, one must not lose sight of the invaluable services rendered to the Lodge of Improvement by the many distinguished Brethren who have occupied the positions of Treasurer and Secretary.

Bro. John Hervey, Grand Secretary, was an active member of Emulation for nearly forty years, and held the Treasurership for many years prior to his death in 1880. He was succeeded by Bro. Thomas Fenn, P.G.D., who held the office until 1894. Bro. Sir Edward Letchworth, Grand

* See Chapter V.

3

Secretary, who had joined Emulation in 1875, succeeded Bro. Fenn, and officiated as Treasurer until 1917, when he was followed by the present Grand Secretary, Bro. Sir Colville Smith. This long and close association between the Lodge of Improvement and Secretaries of the United Grand Lodge is in itself a convincing guarantee of the reliability of Emulation as the recognised standard of English Craft Ritual.

Emulation's Secretaries have numbered many zealous and prominent Freemasons. Comparisons are generally said to be 'odious,' but it must be recorded that no Brother can have rendered greater service to Emulation in this responsible office than Bro. J. Ernest Franck, P.A.G.S.Wks., who retired in January 1931, after holding the position for ten years. He was succeeded by Bro. S. P. Larkworthy, L.R., who was unfortunately compelled for private reasons to relinquish the office after only one year's service. Bro. Larkworthy was followed by Bro. Lieut.-Col. G. P. Orde.

Only those who have been intimately associated with the work of Emulation Lodge of Improvement can form a fair conception of the vast amount of arduous labour falling to the lot of the Secretary and the Assistant Secretary. In the last-mentioned office Bro. Frank W. Simmonds, P.A.G.Reg., has officiated since 1925, and is one of the most popular officials at Headquarters.

On 23rd February 1894, the late Bro. R. Clay

Sudlow, then Leader of Emulation, made the statement:

"We look upon the trust delivered to us as very important indeed—a very sacred one—and speaking for myself, and, I am sure, speaking in the name of my colleagues, I may say that that trust shall be most faithfully, most honourably, and most religiously preserved."

There can be no doubt that a similar spirit animates the members of the Committee of Emulation Lodge of Improvement to-day.

In the course of a speech delivered in 1894 V.W. Bro. Sir Edward Letchworth, then Grand Secretary, stated that the records of Grand Lodge *conclusively proved that the Emulation Lodge of Improvement was looked upon as the standard of Masonic perfection.*

Eight years later the same eminent Brother wrote:

"The present working of the Emulation Lodge of Improvement is generally accepted as the exemplification of the Ritual so authorised." *

On 2nd March 1923, the M.W. the Pro Grand Master, the Rt. Hon. Lord Ampthill, said in the course of a speech:

"The Emulation Lodge of Improvement has for one hundred years maintained a uniform standard of ritual *which has remained unaltered.*"

On 24th February 1928, the Grand Secretary, V.W. Bro. Sir Colville Smith, stated:

---

* By Grand Lodge in 1816.

"We have to thank the Emulation Lodge of Improvement for maintaining *the standard of ritual* for upwards of a century."

The foregoing brief survey of the history and objects of the Emulation Lodge of Improvement may be sufficient to enable the Masonic tyro to answer the question which heads this chapter. Emulation, he will see, is something more than the mere name given to one particular mode of working; it is the name of a famous Masonic institution the influence of which has spread throughout the length and breadth of the English-speaking Masonic world,—an institution which has, for more than a century, ever kept before it the sole object of preserving and transmitting that system of ritual which received, one hundred and sixteen years ago, the seal of approval from the United Grand Lodge of England.

CHAPTER II

EMULATION AND THE GRAND STEWARDS *

FOR many years it has been the customary procedure for Grand Stewards or Past Grand Stewards to take active part in the work at the Emulation Festivals. The programme at these annual demonstrations usually consists of Lecture-work; the last occasion when a Ceremony formed part of the programme was in 1919, all the offices from Master to Inner Guard being occupied by eminent workers from the Red Apron Lodges.

This intimate and valued association of the Red Apron Lodges with the work of Emulation recalls to mind an interesting parallel between the Emulation Lodge of Improvement and the Grand Stewards' Lodge. By a very large section of the Craft, not only in London and the Provinces, but also in the Overseas Districts, Emulation, as has already been pointed out, is held to be the reliable and authoritative standard of English Craft Ritual and Ceremonial; and, in consequence, the members

* Most of the material contained in this chapter is taken from an article by the author, entitled " An Interesting Parallel," published in the *Masonic Record* (Sept.–Oct. 1928) and reproduced here by courtesy of the Editor of that journal.

of the governing body of Emulation Lodge of Improvement are regarded as the hereditary custodians of the Reconciliation Ritual as it was settled and officially authorised by the Grand Lodge in 1816. Similarly, historical records indicate that for some years prior to and after the Union the Grand Stewards' Lodge was generally looked upon as the recognised examplar and guardian of the accepted ritual. Just as, in the present day, the Emulation Festival is the outstanding ritual demonstration of the year, so, during the decades immediately following the Union, the public demonstrations—or Public Nights, as they were known—held by the Grand Stewards' Lodge, were the pre-eminent exhibitions of Reconciliation working. The purpose of those Public Nights during the first part of the nineteenth century was precisely similar to that of the Emulation Festivals in the twentieth century—to disseminate for the instruction and improvement of the Craft generally the ancient and authorised ritual.

As is well known to all students of the history of our Craft Ritual, for some twenty years after the fusion of the rival Grand Lodges the major part of the instruction in the newly arranged Reconciliation Ceremonies was imparted through the medium of the Masonic Lectures; rehearsal of Ceremonies was comparatively rare. Thus, in presenting the annual demonstrations in Lecture-form, the Emulation Lodge of Improvement is not only following the practice generally — although not invariably — adopted by the Grand Stewards' Lodge in the past, it is also perpetuating the common practice of all the ancient Lodges of Instruction which came into being during the immediate post-Union period, of which Emulation Lodge of Improvement and Stability Lodge of Instruction are to-day the lone survivors.

It is on record that, in 1830, Peter Gilkes (then Leader of the Emulation Committee), when addressing a petition to the Grand Master, emphasised that the Lectures at the Emulation Lodge of Improvement were worked 'according to the custom of the Grand Stewards' Lodge.' The petition continued:—

"We are anxious to promote and diffuse the genuine principles of the Art in a *regular, constitutional manner*, and wishing to excite emulation among the younger Brethren, *and to give such instruction* that when they may have the honour to be appointed to any office, or elected to the chair in a Regular Lodge, they may be fully competent to discharge the important duties of the same with that *correctness and regularity* which is so essential to the well ruling and governing of a Lodge."

From the above extract it is obvious (unless we are to accept the incredible theory that Gilkes embodied deliberate falsehoods in his petition) that the Emulation Lodge of Improvement was, at the period under discussion, giving Masonic *instruction* in what was then generally accepted by all loyal Masons as the *regular, constitutional manner—i.e.* according to the system of the Lodge of Reconciliation—thereby preparing its pupils for the correct discharge of their important duties in the various offices of a Regular Lodge.

Some interesting details concerning the Public Nights held by the Grand Stewards' Lodge are to be found in the history of that Lodge for the period from 1735 to 1920, from the pen of that well-known and reliable Masonic historian, Bro. Albert F. Calvert, P.G.Stwd. Convincing testimony that the Grand Stewards' Lodge—even before the final settlement of the Ritual was arrived at—was loyally adhering to the decisions of the Lodge of Reconciliation is provided in the following extract from the Minutes for 21st December 1814:

"The W.M., Wardens and Deacons favoured the Lodge with the mode of initiating, passing, and raising Masons *according to the plan laid down by the Lodge of Reconciliation.*"

No printed or written version of Ceremonies or Lectures has ever been sanctioned or approved by the Emulation Committee, and an incident referred to by Bro. Calvert suggests that a similar policy existed more than a century ago in the Grand Stewards' Lodge, and that a strictly oral method of teaching was adhered to. Upon the first occasion on which a Lecture was worked in Sections on a

Public Night (December 1820) it was reported to the Worshipful Master that a visiting Brother was:

". . . publicly comparing the same with a written book. Whereupon the Master immediately called the Brother before him and, after demanding the Manuscript, reprimanded the Brother for his misconduct, and stated his intention of communicating the circumstances to the Board of General Purposes."

Many convincing indications are provided by Bro. Calvert that the proceedings at the Grand Stewards' Lodge were in accordance with the plan laid down by the Lodge of Reconciliation. From the Minutes for 18th January 1815 it is seen that Bro. the Rev. Samuel Hemming (who was Master of Reconciliation) accepted the Chaplaincy of the Grand Stewards' Lodge. At this date the members of the Lodge of Reconciliation were still engaged in their deliberations concerning the final settlement of the ritual in accordance with the Articles of Union, and it is a reasonable supposition that Hemming would not have identified himself so prominently with the Grand Stewards' Lodge had he not been convinced that the work there was in strict accord with that particular system which he was then assisting to formulate.

At the Centenary Festival of the Grand Stewards' Lodge, held at Freemasons' Tavern on Wednesday, 9th December 1835, the visiting Brethren included Bro. W. H. White and Bro. Edwards Harper, the joint Grand Secretaries at the time of the Union. It was Bro. Edwards Harper who, in 1818,* wrote to the Master of Lodge 498:

"In referring you to Bro. Gilkes I mentioned he would instruct you in the *correct method adopted since the Union.*"

Twenty-five years later (in 1843) Bro. W. H. White, Grand Secretary, himself a Past Grand Steward,† wrote to the Master of Lodge 523:

"Bro. Gilkes was *fully Master of all the Ceremonies.*"

It seems a logical assumption that these two Grand Secretaries, who testified to Peter Gilkes' outstanding ability as an exponent of Reconciliation Ritual, would not have associated themselves with the Grand Stewards' Lodge unless well satisfied that the proceedings therein were in accordance with the officially authorised system.

Turning to the late Bro. Henry Sadler's *History of the Lodge of Emulation*, No. 21, we find in the Minutes, dated 19th June 1821, the following important entry:

"Bro. J. Deans, Jr., W.M., Bro. J. Robinson, J.W., and Bro. W. H. White, P.M., having signified to the Lodge their intention to form a Lodge of Instruction to be holden at the George and Vulture Tavern, in which Lodge of Instruction the *mode of*

* See Chapter I, p. 28.   † See Chapter I, p. 29.

*working is to conform with that of the Grand Stewards'
Lodge*, and stating their wish to hold their meetings
under the sanction of this Lodge, it was unanimously
resolved that permission be given for the said
Lodge of Instruction to meet under sanction of this
Lodge during pleasure."

It is worthy of notice that the Bro. White here
mentioned was the Grand Secretary, and that
Reconciliation working is not referred to. Instead,
the words used are 'the mode of working is to
conform with that of the Grand Stewards' Lodge.'
Here is cogent evidence that the working of that
famous and representative Lodge was regarded as
authoritative by the Grand Secretary himself, and
that such working was in strict compliance with the
rulings of the Lodge of Reconciliation. It will be
noted that the above entry is dated two years before
the foundation of the Emulation Lodge of Improvement. Therefore, Emulation-working could not
be stated as the standard to be adhered to, and we
have: 'the mode . . . of the Grand Stewards'
Lodge.'

If further proof is needed as to the approval of
the proceedings at the Grand Stewards' Lodge by
the Grand Lodge authorities it is supplied under
dates 1837 and 1849. At the Public Night in the
former year Bro. Edwards Harper, Grand Secretary,
expressed on behalf of the visitors their satisfaction
at the proceedings, and associated himself with
the following motion:

"That cordial thanks are due to the W.M., Officers, and other Members of the Grand Stewards' Lodge for the very able, luminous, and perspicacious manner with which the Lectures of the 2nd and 3rd Degrees have now been worked; thereby affording to the Brethren *instruction and improvement*, which when carried out and followed cannot fail to render the *working of the Craft* worthy of deep admiration and delight."

At the Public Night twelve years later (December 1849) Bro. W. H. White, Grand Secretary, proposed a vote of thanks:

". . . for the admirable way in which the Lectures had been worked."

Additional proof that the working of the Grand Stewards' Lodge in the early decades of the nineteenth century adhered as closely to the plan laid down by the Lodge of Reconciliation as does the working of the Emulation Lodge of Improvement to-day is furnished by the recorded approval of Bro. Stephen Barton Wilson and Bro. Dr Robert T. Crucefix. Bro. Crucefix, who joined the Emulation Lodge of Improvement in 1831, and was one of its warmest supporters until his death in 1850, took a close interest in the work of the Grand Stewards' Lodge. At the Public Night in March 1847 he proposed a vote of thanks for the gratification experienced by the visitors in listening to the working of the Lecture in the First Degree.

The Minutes of the Public Night in March 1861 record that a vote of thanks was passed to the Board of General Purposes:

". . . for their liberality in granting the use of the Temple and Organ without the usual payment."

A parallel with this vote is to be found in the records of the Emulation Lodge of Improvement. At the meeting of Emulation on 22nd November 1861:

"A letter was read from the Grand Secretary informing the Lodge that the Board of General Purposes had granted them the gratuitous use of the Hall and Temple for the Annual Festival on the 29th inst. A vote of thanks to the Board of General Purposes was ordered to be recorded on the Minutes."

In these two entries we have material evidence that at this period the Grand Lodge authorities deemed the Grand Stewards' Lodge and the Emulation Lodge of Improvement worthy of special consideration in connection with the public demonstrations which both were giving for the education of the Craft at large.

At the Public Night of the Grand Stewards' Lodge held in March 1861, referred to above, Bro. Stephen Barton Wilson seconded the vote of thanks to the Officers of the Lodge:

". . . for the very excellent and gratifying manner in which the Lectures had been delivered."

It should be noted that, at this period, Bro. Stephen Barton Wilson had been the Leader of the Emulation Committee for nearly thirty years, and his unstinted approval must surely be accepted as weighty testimony to the reliability of the working of the Grand Stewards' Lodge.

In January 1872 the Brethren of the Grand Stewards' Lodge donated five guineas to the fund for the relief of the three daughters of the late Bro. Stephen Barton Wilson:

". . . in testimony of the appreciation by the Lodge of the eminent services rendered to the Craft by our deceased Brother, as Preceptor for many years of the Emulation and other Lodges of Instruction."

Indication as to the *objects* of the Grand Stewards' Lodge, and of the Grand Master's approval of those objects, is furnished by Bro. Calvert in the following extracts from a memorial addressed by the Lodge to H.R.H. the Duke of Sussex in April 1836:

"It must be wholly unnecessary on our part to trouble your Royal Highness with any observations on the proceedings which particularly characterise the Grand Stewards' Lodge, and on the way in which those proceedings have been conducted. The importance of the Grand Stewards' Lodge to keep alive and in due vigour and purity the *various forms and Landmarks established in the Craft, and which are periodically exhibited and communicated to the Members of the Order at large on the Public Nights of the Lodge*, we are well assured is duly felt by your Royal Highness as the Head of the Craft. . . . Having thus passed a Centenary of its existence with advantage to the Craft and credit to its Members, the Master, Wardens, and Brethren of the Grand Stewards' Lodge are anxious to receive the expression of your Royal Highness' approvation of their proceedings, and as a Testimonial that your Royal Highness is of opinion that the Lodge has laboured since its institution, and not unsuccessfully, to maintain the dignity and purity of Freemasonry, *and to disseminate information among the Craft at large*."

The reply to the memorial was contained in a letter to the Master from the Grand Secretary, conveying the orders of the R.W. Deputy Grand Master, Lord St John Spencer Churchill, who had laid the document before the M.W. Grand Master. Bro. W. H. White wrote:

"His Lordship directs me to say that His Royal Highness has been pleased to express himself well satisfied of the zeal with which the Members of the Grand Stewards' Lodge have at all times exerted themselves *to promote the general interest of the Craft*, and of the manner in which their labours have been conducted *to preserve in due purity the various forms, ceremonies, and Landmarks of the Order*."

In February 1838 the Brethren of the Grand Stewards' Lodge resolved to apply to the Board of

General Purposes to waive the charge of £3 for the use of the New Temple by the Lodge on its Public Nights:

". . . on the ground that such meetings are held *for the purpose of disseminating throughout the Craft at large the legitimate working of the Lectures,* and not for any exclusive purpose for the Lodge itself."

In April 1839 a circular signed by the Master and Secretary of the Grand Stewards' Lodge was sent out to the eighteen Lodges which had the privilege of sending Grand Stewards annually, and to others, from which the following is a noteworthy extract:

"On Public Nights in March and December the Lectures *as handed down by time-honoured Masons* are delivered in the Temple, and are attended on every occasion by a large assembly of the Fraternity —an assembly increasing on each meeting—and the Members are desirous to impress on the minds of the Brethren whom they now address that they consider themselves *as Public Stewards for the observance of the Landmarks of the Order,* holding such duty in trust as representatives of the past, *and always with the hope of handing down the trust reposed in them to all succeeding Stewards.*"

The foregoing paragraph provides a striking parallel with a clause in the speech of the late Bro. Clay Sudlow at the Emulation Festival in February 1894.* On that occasion Bro. Sudlow said:

---

* See Chapter I, p. 35.

"We look upon the trust delivered to us as very important indeed—a very sacred one—and, speaking for myself, and, I am sure, speaking in the name of all my colleagues, I may say that that trust shall be most faithfully, most honourably, and most religiously preserved."

That the Brethren of the Grand Stewards' Lodge spared no efforts to perfect their working at the demonstrations on the Public Nights is shown by the fact that in February 1840 the custom was introduced, after the nomination of the Brethren to work the Lectures at the next Public Night, of fixing two evenings prior to the Public Night for rehearsals of the working. Here we find another parallel with the custom now in vogue at Emulation, save that at the Lodge of Improvement the dates for rehearsal of the Festival work are not fixed in open Lodge, and that they number far more than two.

Nine years later, at a special meeting of the Grand Stewards' Lodge, held in March 1849, the Brethren expressed the opinion:

"That it is expedient, with a view to improving the working of the Lectures on the Public Nights, that at every other meeting some portion, not less than three Sections, should be worked."

By the middle of the nineteenth century the financial affairs of the Grand Stewards' Lodge were giving rise to grave concern, and the Minutes for the meeting in November 1850 record that:

4

"The Secretary stated . . . he had a conversation with the M.W. Grand Master as to the state of the Lodge with respect to the number of its Members, etc., when his Lordship was pleased to express his desire to see the Lodge renovated."

Bro. Calvert relates that with a view to stimulating the interest of the Fraternity *in the working of the ceremonies* it was decided in February 1850 to send out to the Lodges a printed letter, informing the members that the Grand Stewards' Lodge held its Public Nights twice a year:

". . . for the purpose of giving an opportunity *to the Craft in general*, and more particularly to the younger members, of hearing the Lectures delivered *according to ancient form*."

The first and only reference to a Grand Stewards' Lodge of Instruction is contained in an entry in the Lodge Minutes, dated 19th March 1890, when a petition was received from Bro. Gordon Smith, P.G.Stwd., and others, requesting the Lodge to grant sanction for a Lodge of Instruction:

"To enable the members of the eighteen Lodges having the privilege of nominating Grand Stewards to work the Ceremonies of the Craft *in accordance with Emulation Working* for their mutual instruction and improvement."

The Secretary reported that he had written to Bro. Gordon Smith for further particulars and details, but had received no reply.   The W.M. and

Brethren therefore considered that the matter should be left in abeyance.

From the foregoing it is seen that the Grand Stewards' Lodge, which had worked the Masonic Lectures at least as far back as the latter part of the eighteenth century, continued that practice *for the instruction and improvement of the Craft generally* until after the middle of the nineteenth century, in addition to *demonstrating the ceremonies as laid down by the Lodge of Reconciliation*; furthermore, that their demonstrations were approved by Hemming, Crucefix, Harper, White and others—who were *possessed of first-hand knowledge of the precise forms and language agreed upon by the Lodge of Reconciliation*.

The intimate and valued association of the Grand Stewards with the work of Emulation Lodge of Improvement, referred to at the commencement of this chapter, has been maintained for many decades. Among the distinguished Grand Stewards who have been prominent members of the Emulation Committee are Bros. Thomas Fenn, P.G.W., and for ten years President of the Board of General Purposes; J. Udall, P.G.D.; F. Hockley; A. A. Richards, D.G.D.C.; J. A. Rucker, P.G.D.; Robert Grey, P.G.W.; F. T. Rushton; Sir Edward Letchworth, Grand Secretary; J. Russell, P.G.St.B.; J. H. Jenks, P.G.D.; Angus N. Scott, P.A.G.D.C.; and Samuel Chalkley, P.A.G.D.C.

The late Bro. J. S. Granville Grenfell, for fourteen

years Grand Director of Ceremonies, Master of the Grand Stewards' Lodge in 1920, was an avowed supporter of Emulation.

Another prominent Past Master of the Grand Stewards' Lodge who has rendered valued support to Emulation is the present President of the Board of General Purposes, Bro. J. Russell McLaren, who on 20th March 1931 gave a demonstration of the Installation Ceremony at the Lodge of Improvement which was described by expert critics in the Masonic Press as one of the most scholarly and impressive ceremonies heard at Emulation Headquarters for a decade.

The names of other Grand Stewards who have given active support and encouragement to Emulation Lodge of Improvement would make a lengthy list.

The Public Nights of the Grand Stewards' Lodge were discontinued (and never resumed) in 1868. At that period the Emulation Lodge of Improvement had for some forty odd years been carrying on similar work on parallel lines, its leaders imbued with the same loyalty to the decisions of the Grand Lodge, and the same resolve to transmit the ancient and authorised ritual unaltered from generation to generation, as had characterised the rulers of the older body.

There can be little doubt that in the present-day Festival Meetings of the Emulation Lodge of Improvement are to be found an interesting echo of the old Public Nights of the Grand Stewards' Lodge.

CHAPTER III

THE EMULATION LECTURES

THE Masonic Lectures have been referred to at some length in the previous chapter, but the subject is one of sufficient importance to merit further attention. An examination of the Minutes of the Lodge of Promulgation * reveals the following entry under date 13th December 1809:

"Resolved that Deacons (being proved on due examination to be not only ancient but necessary Officers) be recommended."

Prior to that time Deacons had not been considered necessary Officers in Lodges under the Regular Grand Lodge, a fact which furnishes strong presumptive evidence that the Ceremonies at that period contained very little work actually of a ceremonial nature.

The greater part of the work was undoubtedly done by catechism, or, as it is understood to-day, through the medium of the Lectures. The actual Ceremonies were brief. The Ceremony of Initiation —then generally known as the ceremony of Making

* See Chapter I, p. 29.

a Mason—was frequently performed in a separate room, known as the Making Room, after which the Brethren repaired to the Lodge proper for the working of the Lectures.

For the working of the Lectures in the eighteenth century the Brethren usually gathered around trestle-tables, enjoying tobacco and liquid refreshment. Generally the Master's questions were addressed to the Senior Warden. Some were occasionally put to the Junior Warden, but these usually related to the tyling of the Lodge and the examination and admission of visitors. The Office of Inner Guard was then unknown, the duties falling to the lot of the Junior Warden. Sometimes a circular method of working the Lectures was adopted and the questions went round the tables, each Brother answering in turn. After the different Sections the Charges were drunk, generally in punch, and volleys were given with firing-glasses. These records of ancient and interesting customs show that Lecture-working is of great antiquity.

As they are known to-day the Lectures are three in number, and are divided into fifteen Sections, seven in the Lecture of the First Degree, five in the Second Degree, and three in the Third Degree. The Sections are all catechetical in form and contain detailed explanations of the various Ceremonies, combined with many beautifully expressed symbolical references to the higher phases of Masonry and Masonic thought.

The earliest Lectures were apparently arranged about the second decade of the eighteenth century by Bro. Dr James Anderson and Bro. Dr John Desaguliers, but soon afterwards a Bro. Martin Clare (afterwards Deputy Grand Master) was authorised by Grand Lodge to prepare a system of Lectures 'without infringing on the Ancient Landmarks.' Some thirty years later, about 1766, that great and distinguished Mason, Bro. Thomas Dunckerley, was commissioned to prepare a fresh set of Lectures.

Still another eminent Mason who prepared Masonic Lectures was Bro. William Hutchinson, sometimes known as 'the father of Masonic symbolism.' Hutchinson was resident at Barnard Castle, Durham, and, while he worked in the North, Bro. William Preston was similarly employed in the South on a system of Masonic Lectures which soon superseded all others.

At the time of the Union in 1813 it was resolved to revise Preston's Lectures, the duty being entrusted to Bro. the Rev. Dr Samuel Hemming, who made several alterations.

In the previous chapter it has been shown that during the early decades of the nineteenth century the Grand Stewards' Lodge was the only admitted authority for the working of a recognised system of Lectures; and ample evidence has been provided in that chapter to show the intimate link existing between the Grand Stewards' Lodge and the

Emulation Lodge of Improvement. According to reliable Masonic historians the Lectures worked at the Grand Stewards' Lodge were William Preston's Lectures (with few, if any, of Hemming's innovations) as formerly worked by the Lodge of Antiquity, No. 2, William Preston's favourite Lodge. From the close bond of association between the Grand Stewards' Lodge and the Emulation Lodge of Improvement it seems a reasonable assumption that these are the Lectures heard at Emulation to-day.

Further strong evidence in support of this assumption is to be found from a survey of the activities of the United Lodge of Perseverance,* founded in 1818 for the express purpose of teaching the Ceremonies and Lectures according to the plan laid down by the Lodge of Reconciliation. As has been made clear in Chapter I (pp. 27 and 28), there can be no reasonable doubt that the Emulation Lodge of Improvement emanated from the United Lodge of Perseverance; and it is worthy of emphasis that the Brethren of the United Lodge of Perseverance solemnly pledged themselves to a strict adherence to the Ceremonies 'as confirmed by the Grand Lodge of England,' and to the *Lectures* which they described as 'Ancient' in the year 1821. It may be mentioned in passing that these Lectures bear strong resemblance to Lectures known to have been widely used in the eighteenth century.

The system of teaching the principles of Masonry

* See Chapter I, p. 27.

by means of Lecture or catechism was not abandoned at the time of the Union, and examination of the Minutes of the Lodge of Reconciliation * reveals that part of the work in that Lodge was done by means of the Lectures. A study of the Minutes of the early Lodges of Instruction formed during the immediate post-Union period shows that their work was almost entirely confined to the Lectures for some years. The Minutes of the Stability Lodge of Instruction (founded in 1817) mention no work other than the Lectures during the first eighteen years of the Lodge's existence. From the Minutes of the United Lodge of Perseverance it is found that on one hundred and fifteen occasions out of one hundred and thirty nothing but Lecture-work was done. In most of the early Lodges the work was confined to the First Lecture, which may be explained by the fact that in those days a large number of Masons never progressed beyond the Degree of an Entered Apprentice.

The adherence to Lecture-working in those early days is easily to be understood when it is remembered that, save for a small number of eminent Masons of outstanding ability and powerful memory—men such as Peter Gilkes (Leader of Emulation Lodge of Improvement) and Philip Broadfoot (Leader of the Stability Lodge of Instruction)—there were probably few Brethren at that time who were able, quickly and thoroughly, to master the newly

* See Chapter I, p. 26.

arranged Reconciliation Ritual. Doubtless these eminent instructors found that the surest and most convenient method of impressing their teaching on the minds of their pupils was by means of question and answer.

It is scarcely possible to say to-day with any degree of certainty when rehearsal of Ceremonies, as it is now practised, supplanted the old Lecture-form of instruction, and when the old Lecturers—or Lecture-Masters as they were more generally known—gave place to the more modern Preceptors; but, as Lecture-teaching became rarer, so the old expert Lecture-Masters grew fewer, and the Lectures were lost in many directions.

In practically every system of working the Test Questions put to a Candidate for Passing or Raising are merely extracts taken from the Emulation Lectures. When the Master offers to put other questions if any Brother so desires, he is assuming that the Candidate knows the whole of the Lecture. It is interesting to note, too, that in most other workings the explanations of the Tracing Boards are merely extracts from the Emulation Lectures threaded together.

It has been mentioned that in many of the old Lodges of Instruction the Lecture-teaching was mainly confined to the First Lecture for many years. This was not so in the Emulation Lodge of Improvement because, that being a Master Masons' Lodge, it adopted the system of the only other

Master Masons' Lodge—the Grand Stewards' Lodge—and devoted equal or more time to the Lectures in the Second and Third Degrees. Peter Gilkes petitioned the Grand Lodge to authorise and govern the Lectures as they had done the actual Ceremonies, but his effort was, unfortunately, a failure. Unfortunately, because there can be little doubt that many of the changes and elaborations which have crept into the Masonic Ceremonies have come about by importations leaking in from old, unauthorised Lectures.

It is because the Emulation Committee realise the danger of such contamination of the Ceremonies that they give the same scrupulous attention to the teaching of the Lectures to-day as did their predecessors in the past, and insist that any Brother elected to the Committee must be an expert Lecture-Master. The leakage of Lecture-work into the Ceremonies has ever been a danger to the purity of the ancient ritual; only by constant comparison and study of the two, Lectures and Ceremonies together, can the danger be averted. In no other School of Masonic Instruction is the safeguard so rigidly maintained as at the Emulation Lodge of Improvement.

CHAPTER IV

THE EMULATION MATCH-BOX

PROBABLY no feature in connection with Emulation Lodge of Improvement has been made the subject of more disparaging criticism than the famous silver match-box, the award presented by the Committee to a Brother who succeeds in working any one of the Ceremonies at the Lodge of Improvement without error in either word or action. Both in speech and in writing, unfriendly critics have referred glibly to the introduction of a 'pot-hunting spirit' into the study of Masonic Ritual.

Such criticism can only emanate from those who are woefully ignorant of their subject and totally unfamiliar with the true spirit which influences the great majority of the regular workers at Emulation Headquarters. The significant fact that Brethren who have secured the coveted guerdon for perfect rendering of *all* the Ceremonies continue to figure among Emulation's most loyal and regular supporters should afford convincing proof to all save the most biased of critics that Emulation's hold upon the enthusiasm of its adherents is based upon a foundation far more secure and enduring than any mere thought of securing a tangible reward for their labours.

A few there may be who are actuated by the desire to possess a material symbol of their ritualistic proficiency; that is, perhaps, inevitable. But an intimate association with Emulation extending over many years has convinced the present writer that the sudden withdrawal of the famous match-box would lessen Emulation's popularity not a jot, and that the vast majority of the workers at the Lodge of Improvement are inspired by genuine interest in and love for the Masonic Ritual, combined with a commendable desire to assist, individually and collectively, in preserving and propagating that which they conscientiously believe to be the ancient and authorised form of working as settled by the Lodge of Reconciliation. Any spirit of rivalry that may be engendered at Emulation by the silver match-box is a spirit of rivalry in its healthiest sense. The box, when won, is not regarded as a trophy, but rather as a visible emblem of industry, faith, and perseverance—the outward token of a Brother's belief that a Masonic Ceremony is a Solemn Rite of such vital importance as to be worthy of performance with dignified accuracy and such perfection as humans may hope to attain.

For seventy-four years the match-box was unknown at Emulation Lodge of Improvement. Its creation came about by mere chance. It was in the autumn of 1897 that a well-known member of

Emulation, Bro. R. L. Badham, worked the Second Ceremony without correction, an effort which was afterwards the subject of comment by the late Bro. R. Clay Sudlow, Emulation's Leader for thirty years. Bro. Sudlow's comment was a casual one, but the happening was evidently sufficiently unusual as to leave an impression on his mind. Shortly afterwards he asked Bro. Badham's acceptance of a little memento of his performance in the form of a silver match-box. Such was the birth of what has since become a world-famous Masonic emblem.

For some years Bro. Sudlow was the personal donor of the Emulation match-box. At the Festival held under the Presidency of R.W. Bro. Sir Augustus Webster, Prov. G.M., Hants and the Isle of Wight, on 7th March 1902, Bro. Sudlow stated in the course of a speech:

"I may say that the apotheosis of an absolutely correct working of a Ceremony in the Emulation Lodge of Improvement is a silver match-box, upon which is recorded the success achieved; and so frequently nowadays is that distinction won that the giver may yet live to find himself in the Bankruptcy Court."

On presentation the Emulation match-box bears an inscription with the name of the Brother receiving it, the Ceremony he worked, and the date. A subsequent success earns a further inscription, known colloquially among Emulation-workers as a

'scratch.' After perfect working of all the Ceremonies the words 'Complete Record' are added.

For some eight years after its inception the box
could be won for accurate working of the First
Ceremony without the Charge, or the Second
Ceremony without the T.B.   The Complete Record,
however, could not be obtained until these Ceremonies had been accurately demonstrated in their
entirety.   It was therefore possible for a Complete
Record-holder's box to bear six 'scratches.'   Only
two such records were ever completed, one by the
late Bro. J. F. Roberts, P.A.G.D.C., whose match-
box may be seen in the Grand Lodge Museum.

That the Emulation match-box is no easy prize
may be judged by the number which have been won
during the thirty-five years which have elapsed
since the award was instituted. Exactly 166
Brethren have been successful in passing the test,
an average of approximately 4·7 per year.   Of these
the following 51 Brethren have the distinction
of being Complete Record-holders:

Charles Lewis .	. 1900	J. J. Black .	. 1912
R. E. F. Lander	. 1900	J. Kelly White .	. 1913
M. V. Cassall .	. 1903	A. N. Scott .	. 1913
T. Allsop .	. 1904	F. W. Giles .	. 1913
J. F. Roberts .	. 1904	R. A. Doble .	. 1914
F. W. Byles .	. 1906	R. S. Neumann	. 1914
S. W. Heaton .	. 1906	W. Pragnell .	. 1914
F. O'C. Slingo .	. 1908	D. Ingamells .	. 1916
L. H. Dear .	. 1909	A. B. Wilson .	. 1916
J. Crouch. .	. 1909	S. A. Knaggs .	. 1917
H. C. Dodson .	. 1912	N. Colbeck .	. 1917
F. C. Schultz .	. 1912	C. Newell .	. 1918

J. H. Earls	.	1919	A. Macdonald .	. 1928
C. H. Slack	.	1919	H. W. Bangert .	. 1928
G. Paxon	.	1921	T. U. Batcheldor	. 1928
A. J. Peyton	.	1921	R. H. Smith .	. 1928
H. C. Tasker .		1924	G. Derrick .	. 1929
A. M. Shepherd		1924	H. R. Donaldson	. 1930
H. B. J. Franklin		1924	T. J. Norman .	. 1930
S. P. Larkworthy		1925	H. W. Goldfinch	. 1931
Herbert F. Inman		1925	G. F. Goodspeed	. 1931
A. Sharp . .		1925	H. J. Paterson .	. 1931
F. P. Reynolds .		1925	A. W. Powell .	. 1932
P. de Worms .		1926	L. P. More .	. 1932
C. J. Chapman .		1927	H. A. Rowbotham	. 1932
W. G. Hamilton		1928		

CHAPTER V

THE EMULATION COMMITTEE

IN a previous chapter it has been shown that from its foundation in 1823 the Emulation Lodge of Improvement has never been under the control of an individual Preceptor, but has always been ruled by a Committee of experienced instructors selected by the general body of members from amongst the most expert of their number. For some ninety years the ruling Committee consisted of three trusted Past Masters, exclusive of the Treasurer and Secretary. In 1914 a fourth member was added, and the Committee remained at that strength for twelve years. In 1926 it was increased to six.

During the one hundred and nine years which have elapsed since the foundation of the Lodge of Improvement appointments to the Committee have been of sufficient rarity to excite widespread interest throughout the Craft. This is at once apparent from a study of the Emulation Minute Books dating back to 1859. The records prior to that date were unfortunately destroyed, but those available reveal the interesting information that the majority of the Brethren elected to the Committee during the last

5

seventy years have served thereon for periods ranging from ten to twenty years. Consequently but few Brethren, however competent they may be as instructors, can ever hope to receive the distinction of election to the Committee of the Emulation Lodge of Improvement.

The fact that the long list of Lodges of Instruction affiliated to the Lodge of Improvement includes Lodges working in New Zealand, South America, India, South Africa, China, Malay Straits, West Indies, Gibraltar, Egypt, East and West Africa, and on the Continent of Europe, affords ample evidence that the personnel of the Emulation Committee must necessarily be a matter of considerable importance among Freemasons, not only in London and the Provinces, but also to Brethren in far-away Districts in all parts of the world.

In response to many suggestions received since publication of the first edition of this Manual the following details are appended relating to the present members of the Emulation Committee:—

G. J. V. RANKIN, P.G.D.

Bro. George John Valler Rankin was born in November 1856, and initiated at the age of thirty-five in the Crichton Lodge, 1641, in 1891. A Founder and first Senior Warden of the Kirby Lodge, 2818, in 1900, he was installed as Master in 1901. The following year he was appointed

Secretary, holding the office for ten years. He was then elected as Treasurer, filling that office till 1924, when he served a second period as Master. On vacating the chair he was again elected to the Treasurership, which office he still holds. A joining member of the Columbia Lodge, 2397, he served as Master in 1902 and 1918, and has been Secretary for many years. In the Thomas Ralling Lodge, 2508, he ruled as Master in 1904. He was a Founder and first Master of the Joseph Lancaster Lodge, 3439, in 1910. In 1914 he was appointed A.G.D.C., being promoted to the rank of P.G.D. ten years later. He has been a member of the Board of General Purposes since 1911.

Contrary to general belief, Bro. Rankin was not, at the beginning of his Masonic career, an adherent to the Emulation system of working; his first Masonic knowledge was derived from a Lodge of Instruction in the South-East of London. At the Emulation Festivals in 1900, 1901, 1902, and 1903 he occupied a Warden's chair. He secured the Emulation Match-box for accurate rendering of the First Ceremony (without the Charge) in 1899, and was equally successful with the same Ceremony in its entirety in 1901. In 1902 he gave an accurate rendering of the Second Ceremony, exclusive of the T.B.

Bro. Rankin joined the Lodge of Improvement in 1895, and was appointed to the Committee in 1904, having previously acted for six years as

Preceptor of the Kirby L.I. In 1914 he succeeded the late Bro. Clay Sudlow as Leader of the Committee. He has therefore held the Leadership for nineteen years, and it may fairly be said that his period of rule has marked the most successful epoch in Emulation's history.

J. J. Black, P.A.G.D.C.

Bro. John Joseph Black may fairly be described as Emulation's veteran whom "age cannot wither nor custom stale." Born on 6th February 1851, he was initiated in the St John's Lodge, 1564, on his thirty-first birthday, 6th February 1882. In the same year he joined Emulation Lodge of Improvement, and he can therefore claim a far longer personal knowledge of Emulation ritual and procedure than any of his colleagues.

He was installed Master of the St John's Lodge in November 1886, less than five years after his initiation, and was re-elected for a second period of office till January 1888, the month of Installation being changed at that period. From January 1888 till December 1918 he served as Secretary. In January 1906 he joined the Wey Side Lodge, 1395, acting as Master in 1909; he has been Secretary of that Lodge since 1910.

In 1916 he was appointed Past Assistant Grand Director of Ceremonies. A prominent worker in the Province of Surrey, he was appointed Provincial

Grand Deacon in 1898, and promoted to Provincial Grand Warden in 1910. In 1887 he was mainly responsible for the formation of the Woking Emulation Lodge of Improvement.

Often referred to affectionately as the 'Father' of Emulation, Bro. Black proved himself a ritualist of outstanding ability soon after joining the Lodge of Improvement, where he holds the Complete Record for perfect working of all the Ceremonies. As a Lecture-worker in the 'eighties and 'nineties his record was unequalled; he was selected to work at nine Emulation Festivals between 1883 and 1894. He was elected a member of the Headquarters Committee in 1913.

S. A. KNAGGS, P.A.G.D.C.

Bro. Sydney Angelo Knaggs was initiated in the Chère Reine Lodge, 2853, of which Lodge he is a Past Master. He is also a Past Master of the St Mary's Lodge, 63. For many years he was a Preceptor of the St Luke's Medical Lodge of Instruction and a member of the Committee of the Kirby Lodge of Instruction. A ritualist of unusual ability, he came into prominence as a worker at the Lodge of Improvement soon after he joined in 1910. Securing the match-box for perfect rendering of the Second Ceremony and T.B. in 1914, he repeated his success the following year with the First and Third Ceremonies. In 1917 he achieved the Complete Record with a flawless demonstration of the Ceremony of Installation. He was appointed G.St.B. in 1923, and promoted to P.A.G.D.C. in 1929.

Bro. Knaggs was appointed to the Emulation Committee in 1920 and is, perhaps, its most popular representative among the rank and file of the members. As rigidly accurate in matters of ritual as any of his colleagues, he combines with his inflexibility of teaching a kindly spirit of understanding and a fraternal tolerance for the failings of less expert Brethren. If, in the ordinary course of events, he succeeds to the Leadership at Emulation, as it may be assumed that he will, it is a sure prophecy that he will discharge the duties of that responsible office with ability, dignity, and that complete absence of self-conceit which marks the true Leader.

A. B. WILSON, P.A.G.D.C.

Bro. Arthur Bernard Wilson was initiated in the Burlington Lodge, 96, on 13th November 1906, and installed as Master on 4th March 1913. He is a joining member and Past Master of the St Mary's Lodge, 63. He received the rank of P.A.G.D.C. in 1924. Joining Emulation Lodge of Improvement in 1907, he became a prominent worker there about two years later. In 1915 he secured the silver match-box, giving perfect demonstrations of the

Ceremonies of Raising and Installation during that year. The following year he obtained the Complete Record with accurate expositions of the Ceremonies of Initiation and Passing.

In 1912 Bro. Wilson was appointed (in co-operation with Bro. Knaggs) to the Preceptorship of the St Luke's Medical Lodge of Instruction. In 1920 he became Preceptor of the Navy Lodge of Instruction, holding that office until his preferment to the Headquarters Committee in 1926. He is a fluent speaker with a command of apt and picturesque metaphor and a happy gift for saying 'the right thing' at all times.

A. J. PEYTON, P.M. 2128

Bro. Archibald John Peyton has the distinction of being the only member of the Emulation Committee wearing a light-blue apron. He was initiated in the United Northern Counties Lodge, 2128, on 1st February 1910, but did not reach the Master's chair till December 1919, his Masonic advancement being interrupted by military service. Joining the Langton Lodge of Instruction in 1912, he was appointed to the Committee in 1914, serving thereon until 1920. From January 1922 until April 1924 he officiated as Preceptor of the Wolsey Lodge of Instruction. He became Preceptor of the Ad Astra Lodge of Instruction in 1924, having previously served as Deputy Preceptor for three years.

Bro. Peyton joined the Emulation Lodge of Improvement in 1920, and at once became noticed as a worker of conspicuous ability. At his initial attempt he secured the silver match-box for perfect rendering of the First Ceremony in 1920, repeating his success with the Ceremonies of Passing, Raising, and Installation in 1921. He was elected to the Emulation Committee in 1929.

H. C. Tasker, P.P.G.Reg., Middx.

Bro. Harold Charles Tasker was born on 15th August 1875, and initiated in the Campbell Lodge, 1415, in 1912. He served as Master in 1917. In 1924 he was appointed Provincial Grand Registrar, Middlesex. He was Preceptor of the Campbell Lodge of Instruction from 1913 till 1929, and of the City Liveries Lodge of Instruction from 1923 till 1929.

Bro. Tasker joined Emulation Lodge of Improvement in 1921, and secured the silver match-box for accurate demonstration of the Second and Third Ceremonies in 1922. In 1923 he gave a perfect rendering of the First Ceremony, and was equally successful with the Ceremony of Installation in 1924. He therefore shares with all his colleagues (except Bro. Rankin) the distinction of holding the Complete Record for perfect demonstration of all the Emulation Ceremonies. He was elected to the Headquarters Committee in January 1930.

CHAPTER VI

SQUARING THE LODGE

THE adverse criticism most frequently heard concerning Emulation-working is with regard to the absence of 'squaring' of the Lodge each time an Officer or Member has to move from one part of the Lodge to another. One frequently hears such statements as: "I don't like Emulation, it is slovenly because they *never* square the Lodge."

Such a criticism can only be said to be born of sheer ignorance, but it is noticeable that many of the most trenchant criticisms of the Emulation system come from Brethren who have never been inside the Emulation Lodge of Improvement in their lives and who are, therefore, scarcely fitted to assume the rôle of critics. Careful perusal of Chapters XVI and XVII, relating to the duties of the Junior and Senior Deacons, will show that scrupulous attention is given to 'squaring' the Lodge in the Emulation Ceremonies—on those occasions when 'squaring' is necessary.

Freemasonry, we are taught, is a 'peculiar system of morality veiled in allegory and illustrated by symbols.' The 'squaring' of the Lodge has its symbolism during the actual progress of a Ceremony. At an early stage of the Ceremony of Initiation the Master proclaims that the Brethren from the N., E., S., and W. will take notice that the Candidate is about to pass in view before them to show that he *is* the Candidate properly prepared, and a fit and proper person to be made a Mason. The Candidate has, therefore, to be conducted by the Junior Deacon *via* the N. to the E., and thence by way of the S. to the W. There is here both a symbolical and a logical reason for 'squaring' the Lodge, and it *is* so 'squared.' Similarly at a later stage in the Ceremony and at certain stages in the subsequent Ceremonies.

At that point in each Ceremony where the Candidate is directed by the Master to retire for the purpose of restoring himself to his p.c.'s there is no longer any need for 'squaring.' That particular portion of the Ceremony is then *completed*, the Candidate has merely to retire from the Lodge and there is no reason, either symbolical or logical, why ceremonial 'squaring' should be indulged in. Nor does any such reason exist when Brother Secretary or Brother Director of Ceremonies may have occasion to move from one part of the Lodge to another in the execution of duties quite apart from the actual Ceremonies.

Generally speaking, it may be laid down that in the Emulation Ceremonies the Lodge is *always* 'squared' when the Candidate in charge of the

Deacon is actually taking part in a ceremonial or symbolical portion of the work. At other times the Lodge is not so 'squared,' and those who are so quick adversely to criticise Emulation-working on that account may well pause to reflect that, in the eyes of others, their own perpetual 'squaring' of the Lodge may perchance appear to be superfluous, and perhaps a little ridiculous.

The author has to confess that he has not yet been able to find a Brother who could offer him a logical and convincing reason for 'squaring' every time one moves in Lodge. The custom would appear to be based on no greater authority or reason than that which governs the habit of passing the port-decanter in one particular direction at dinner.

CHAPTER VII

SOME DIFFERENCES OF WORKING

AFTER the troublesome question regarding the 'squaring' of the Lodge, the criticism most frequently advanced against Emulation-working is that it is 'curt' and 'discourteous,' because an Officer is not taught to show the Sn. on every occasion when he is addressed by a senior Officer during a Ceremony. In nearly all other modes of working such is the accepted practice.

It is not the purpose of this chapter to argue the question, but rather to offer advice for the guidance of Brethren who, although desirous of adhering to Emulation procedure, rarely or never attend a recognised Emulation-working Lodge of Instruction, and are consequently in doubt as to when the Sn. should be used. Unfortunately their number is legion, and for such Brethren a simple 'rule-of-thumb' direction must be found if possible.

Perhaps the surest guide with regard to the use of the Sn. in Emulation-working is to remember that a junior does *not* show the Sn. when addressed by a senior, nor when merely replying to a question, but that he *always* salutes when he himself has cause to address a senior Officer.

A simple illustration may be found in the Ceremony of Closing the Lodge. The W.M. addresses the J.W.: 'Bro. J.W., w.i.t.c.c.o.e.M.?' The J.W. is *being addressed* and does *not* show the Sn. when replying: 'T.p.t.L.c.t.' He is instructed to direct that duty to be done and addresses the I.G.: 'Bro. I.G., p.t.L.c.t.' The I.G., *being spoken to*, does *not* salute. The I.G., having discharged his duty at the door, returns to position, and he now has to address a senior Officer. He should take the Sp. and show the Sn. The J.W. in his turn has now to make a report to the W.M., he has to *address him*, not merely reply to a question. Therefore, after proper use of his ━┫, he takes Sp. and stands to O. before speaking. So the rule is: When *spoken to* or when merely replying to a question, no Sn. by the junior Officer: when *deliberately addressing* a senior, then the Sn. *is* used.

The above direction applies, of course, only during an actual Ceremony; Emulation has no claims, historical or otherwise, to issue rulings for the conduct of Brethren outside the actual Ceremonies. At all other times, when addressed by the Master, a Brother should show courtesy to the chair by rising and standing to O.

A very similar point of difference between Emulation-working and other systems is to be found in the S.W.'s work. In the majority of systems the S.W. springs to his feet and shows the Sn. when addressed by the W.M. during a Ceremony. In

Emulation the S.W. will not go far wrong if he remembers to remain seated when addressed, but to stand to O. when he has to address the Master. For example, after the W.M. has 'addressed a few questions to the Can.' at an early stage during the Initiation Ceremony, he addresses the S.W.: 'Bro. S.W., you will direct the J.D. to instruct the Can. . . .' The S.W., *being addressed*, remains seated. At an earlier point, when the S.W. has to present: 'Mr A.B., a Can. properly prepared . . .' he stands to O. with the Sp. and Sn.

A third point where Emulation differs from the majority of workings, and where Brethren who are infrequent in their attendance at Lodge of Instruction are often at fault, is in connection with the Deacons' work. In most systems the Deacon shows the Sn. whenever the Can. does so. In Emulation-working this is *never* done. Can there be a more undignified sight than to see a Deacon waving his wand about while endeavouring to salute the W.M. 'in passing'? Every Masonic salute should be given with smart, military precision, and never with any implement in the hand.

Deacons who may be uncertain on the point as to whether they should halt a Can. before directing him to salute at the W.M. or W.'s pedestals should remember that in Emulation-working a salute is *never* given 'in passing.' (See footnote on p. 146.)

In many modes of working it is customary for the W.M. to give ▬▬▌ and for all the Brethren to rise at the words 'In G.' during the Charge after the Initiation, a proceeding which probably results in distracting the Can.'s attention in the middle of a solemn address to which he should be applying his mind intently. This interruption of the Charge should never occur in an Emulation Ceremony.

Two points in the Third Degree sometimes give rise to uncertainty in the minds of would-be Emulation-workers who do not attend their Lodge of Instruction. The first is as to whether the s...t should be open or folded during a certain part of the Ceremony. The s...t should *never* be folded. The second doubt which frequently arises is with regard to the correct point for restoring the L.'s. This should not be done until after the Can. has retired to restore himself to h.p.c.'s. (See footnote on p. 148.)

In some modes of working the W.M. returns a salute when saluted by an Officer or the Can., retaining his seat while he does so. In Emulation-working the W.M. will not err if he remembers that the Sn. is *never* returned. In any case no Masonic Sn. can correctly be given *while seated*. In every Degree a Can. is carefully instructed regarding the position in which 'the S.'s of the Deg. are com.' A Sn. *is* a Masonic S.

In the majority of systems the Sn. shown by the Brethren during an Ob. in any Degree is the Sn. of F. In Emulation (and Stability) the Brethren show the P. Sn. of the particular Degree in which the

Lodge is working. Certainly it seems incongruous that the Sn. of F., which belongs to the Second Degree, should be employed during the First and Third Degrees. Emulation and Stability, being the only two systems of working which can advance definite and reasonable claims to direct descent from the authorised working of the Lodge of Reconciliation, as sanctioned by the United Grand Lodge in 1816, it would appear to be a reasonable assumption that they are adhering to the ancient and regular custom in employing the P. Sn. of the Degree during an Ob.

During the Explanation of the Second T.B. references are made to the 'middle chamber of the Temple.' Emulation-workers who aim at word-perfection are often at a loss to remember the two occasions when the words 'of the Temple' should be omitted. An infallible 'rule-of-thumb' is to remember that they are omitted when the word 'arrived' is employed. 'After our ancient Brethren had entered the porch they *arrived . . .* which led to the *middle chamber.*' 'After our ancient Brethren had gained the summit of the winding staircase they *arrived* at the door of the *middle chamber.*' In these two instances only, omit the words 'of the Temple.'

Many other cases of difference of working which give rise to confusion among inexperienced workers might be cited, but the foregoing are among the most frequent. The rulings given are, of course, in conformity with strict Emulation procedure, but Brethren will be wise to remember that in Masonry, as in other spheres of life, there is much wisdom in the ancient fragment of advice: "When in Rome, do as the Romans do."

However ardent a believer in Emulation practice a younger Brother may be, he will be ill-advised to endeavour to *thrust* that practice upon his Lodge when it is obviously unwelcome to the majority of the Brethren. If his enthusiasm is such that he cannot bring himself to abide by the avowed and desired system of the majority of his Brethren, then his only proper course is to resign and seek membership in more congenial company in an Emulation-working Lodge.

If it is 'unwise' for an Emulation enthusiast to endeavour to thrust his favoured system unduly upon his own Lodge, it is far worse for him to adopt such an attitude when he is a *guest* in another Lodge. Unfortunately it sometimes happens, but such over-zealous enthusiasts will do well to remember that such conduct is a disservice to Emulation, and that Masonic harmony and fraternal toleration are of greater value and more vital importance than conspicuous and sometimes rather ill-mannered insistence upon one's own particular beliefs.

6

PART II

THE OFFICERS OF THE LODGE
AND THEIR DUTIES

THE OFFICERS OF THE LODGE
AND THEIR DUTIES

RULE 129, *Book of Constitutions*, states that the regular Officers of a Lodge consist of the Master and his two Wardens, a Treasurer, a Secretary, two Deacons, an Inner Guard, and a Tyler. The Master may also appoint a Chaplain, a Director of Ceremonies, an Assistant Director of Ceremonies, an Almoner, an Organist, an Assistant Secretary, and Stewards.

The table of precedence is as follows:—

*1.—The Worshipful Master.
*2.—The Senior Warden.
*3.—The Junior Warden.
 4.—The Chaplain.
*5.—The Treasurer.
*6.—The Secretary.
 7.—The Director of Ceremonies.
*8.—The Senior Deacon.
*9.—The Junior Deacon.
10.—The Assistant Director of Ceremonies.

* Those marked with an asterisk are the 'Regular' or necessary Officers of the Lodge, while the remainder are the 'Permissive' Officers whom the Master *may* appoint if he so desires.

11.—The Almoner.
12.—The Organist.
13.—The Assistant Secretary.
*14.—The Inner Guard.
15.—The Stewards.
*16.—The Tyler.

* See footnote on p. 85.

CHAPTER VIII

THE TYLER

" To all poor and distressed Masons, wherever dispersed over the face of earth and water."

So runs the familiar "Tyler's Toast," and it should be remembered that Brother Tyler himself is frequently to some extent a poor and distressed Brother, perchance a worthy old Past Master who, having fallen upon hard times, is glad to retain active association with the Craft, and at the same time to receive the emoluments of his Office.

" He who is placed on the lowest spoke of Fortune's wheel is equally entitled to our regard." Such is the reminder to be found in the Fifth Section of the First Lecture; while, in the final Section of the Third Lecture, it is impressed upon our minds that *"the word Brother among Masons is something more than a name."*

Let us not forget then that, even though Brother Tyler may be a serving Brother, we meet him on the Square and part from him on the Level. A fraternal word of greeting, accompanied by a handshake, will possibly be valued even more than a piece of silver in the 'plate,' and, if Brother Tyler has been wisely chosen for his Office, our friendly overtures are not likely to be abused.

Brother Tyler may truthfully claim that his Office is one of antiquity. He was first mentioned in Grand Lodge Minutes under date 8th June 1732, and reference to his Office is to be found in the Constitutions of 1738. He cannot be 'appointed' by the Worshipful Master, sharing as he does with Brother Treasurer the distinction of being an 'elected' Officer of the Lodge. Once elected he may, if he be trustworthy and diligent, confidently look forward to re-election from year to year, for there is little likelihood of any Lodge dispensing with the services of a good Tyler.

That Brother Tyler should be a man of unimpeachable character, tact, and courteous demeanour is essential, for not only is he brought into contact with distinguished Brethren who are visiting the Lodge, but, by the very nature of his duties, he is the first Officer of the Lodge to have any ceremonial dealings with a Candidate seeking admission to our Order. The ceremony to take place within the Lodge is one of solemnity and beauty, and it is not to be imagined that Brother Tyler would indulge in anything in the nature of jocularity with the Candidate in the preparation-room.

In some Lodges it is customary for the Worshipful Master to depute the Director of Ceremonies, or some other Brother of ability, to assist with the preparation of the Candidate; but for the purpose of this Manual it is assumed that the Tyler is thoroughly competent to superintend such details, as, indeed, he usually is. Likewise, it is assumed that he has long since acquired word-perfection in the phrasing of the reports for the various Degrees.

It is quite likely that our Brother Tyler was well versed in the mysteries of the Craft before our attention was first directed to the Three Great Lights. We assume, therefore, that we are not here writing for the guidance of a younger Brother, and it is not proposed to discuss the duties of the Tyler's Office in detail. Suffice it to say that those duties may truthfully be described as multifarious; the Tyler who discharges them in a thoroughly conscientious and efficient manner will earn the lasting gratitude and goodwill of Brother Secretary and Brother Director of Ceremonies, who will certainly find themselves relieved of much anxiety in connection with minor details.

If there be one direction in which confusion is apt to arise in relation to the Tyler's duties it is with respect to the series of reports given upon the door of the Lodge. If such confusion arises let us not be too hasty in condemnation of the Brother who guards the outer porch, for it has to be remembered that he serves many Lodges and that Masonic customs vary in this connection as in others. We who believe in one particular system should not be too ready to condemn all others as wrong.

In many Lodges, more particularly in the Provinces, differentiation is made between a 'Report' and an 'Alarm,' the former (consisting of the K.'s of the Degree in which the Lodge is working) being used for a Member of the Lodge or for a well-known Visitor, while the latter (consisting of a single K.) is used in the case of a stranger seeking admission. There may be much to be said both for and against the practice, but the fact remains that the single K. *has no Masonic significance.* In the Emulation system of working, with which we are here more particularly concerned, no such report is countenanced.

Where single K.'s or 'Alarms' are the practice this method of report is generally used to announce the presence of a Candidate for Initiation, but here it would seem that there *is reasonable objection* to be advanced. Ritual may not be *binding,* but the indisputable fact remains that, in the Second Section of the First of the Ancient Lectures, there is to be found the statement that the Candidate gains admission to the Lodge by means of *three distinct K.'s,* which K.'s allude to the ancient and venerable exhortation: "*Seek and ye shall find, ask and ye shall have, knock and it shall be opened unto you.*"

When a Candidate for Passing awaits admission the K.'s of the First Degree are given indicating to the Brethren within the Lodge that a Brother below the Degree of a F.C. is without. In like manner when a Candidate for Raising is seeking admission the K.'s of a F.C. are given to indicate that a Brother below the Degree of a M.M. is without. As already stated, the single K. has no Masonic significance; therefore, when the Candidate is one for Initiation, the K.'s of the First Degree must be given. At Emulation Lodge of Improvement, however, a slight difference is made (possibly for the information of the I.G. and J.W.), the K.'s for a Candidate being given by the Tyler rather heavier and more deliberately than in the case of an ordinary report.

Perhaps the best advice that can be tendered to Brother Tyler is that he should familiarise himself with the custom of each particular Lodge, thus avoiding confusion and possible irritation.

A useful service may be rendered by Bro. Tyler when a Can. is dismissed from the Lodge to restore himself to his p.c.'s in any Degree. It is to see that the Can. knows how to take the Sp. and give the Sn. correctly when readmitted. In the Third Degree it may be taken for granted that the Can. certainly will *not* know what is expected of him. If Bro. Tyler would take this excellent opportunity of imparting a little fraternal instruction, both Can.'s and S.D.'s would be saved much confusion, and the Can.'s re-entry would be a smoother and more dignified happening than is the general rule.

For an hour or more before the time for the opening of the Lodge the Tyler will probably be busy. Furniture and regalia have to be properly arranged, the anteroom prepared, and various details attended to so that all may be in readiness for the Secretary on his arrival. A little later it is Brother Tyler who is generally held responsible for seeing that signatures are entered in the Attendance Book by Members and Visitors. Many other demands are made upon him. The Lodge being closed, furniture and regalia have to be collected and locked safely away, after which the Tyler's services are probably required in the dining-room. The first to arrive, he is the last to leave. Altogether it may fairly be said that he is one of the hardest-worked Officers of the Lodge.

Bearing in mind the words of our Brother the Senior Warden during the closing of the Lodge, let those of us who are more fortunately placed see to it at the close of each happy evening that Brother Tyler 'has had his due.'

CHAPTER IX

THE STEWARD

THE young Mason who is appointed a Steward is taking his first active step on the long journey which will lead him, it is to be hoped, to the exalted position occupied by the Master in the East. If there be but one Steward appointed in his Lodge the journey is not such a long one, after all, and the newly appointed Steward may reasonably hope that it will be his good fortune to win promotion to the Office of Inner Guard in the near future.

Rule 129, *Book of Constitutions*, however, sets no limit on the number of Stewards whom the Master *may* appoint. It is not uncommon in large Lodges for the Master to appoint four or six Stewards, although, be it noted, no such appointment as *Senior* or *Junior* Steward is permissible, still less that of *Wine* Steward.*

In Lodges where several Stewards are appointed the Brother receiving his first Collar of Office must perforce look forward to a lengthy period of appren-

* The term *Wine Steward* should never be employed. The author has in mind an incident at a Consecration Meeting when the newly installed Master was admonished by the Grand Secretary for employing the term.

ticeship; he will be well advised to utilise this interval by fitting himself for the more important duties which may perchance fall to his lot sooner than he anticipates.

In theory the duties of Brother Steward, as sometimes explained to him by the Worshipful Master, include '*introducing visitors and seeing that they are properly accommodated,*' '*assisting in the collection of dues and subscriptions,*' and '*generally assisting the Deacons and other Officers in performing their respective duties.*' In practice Brother Steward will probably find that the '*introduction of visitors*' is a duty attended to by Brother Director of Ceremonies and his Assistant, that the '*collection of dues and subscriptions*' is solely a matter for Brother Treasurer and Brother Secretary, and that the Deacons and other Officers require little or no assistance in '*performing their respective duties.*'

At the same time Brother Steward should not lose sight of the fact that he *is* an Officer of the Lodge and that he may make himself a very useful one. It frequently happens that an Officer is absent, in which case it is the Steward who should be qualified to fill the vacancy, a qualification which he can only attain by diligent attendance at a Lodge of Instruction.

Thus it may well happen that the recently appointed Steward may even find himself in the proud position of occupying a Warden's chair if he has familiarised himself with the work. In this connection it has somewhere been written that no Brother is eligible to occupy a Warden's chair in a regular Lodge unless he shall have been regularly appointed to that high Office. There appears to be no reliable authority for such a pronouncement. The present writer well remembers an occasion in his Masonic youth when he acted in such a capacity long before he had received even the junior appointment of Steward.

From the foregoing it will be seen that Brother Steward need not think that his duties are entirely limited to ministering to the wants of his Brethren during the period of Refreshment, although such duty is one he must be prepared to undertake cheerfully and to discharge efficiently. The proportion of responsibility which will rest upon him in this connection depends largely upon Lodge custom. In many Lodges it is the Treasurer or Secretary who controls such matters as the consumption of wine and the expenditure with regard to refreshment. It is possible, too, that the Director of Ceremonies prefers to attend to the accommodation and seating of the guests.

The best advice which can be offered to Brother Steward is that he should show himself ready and willing at all times to render all possible assistance to his Senior Officers both at Labour and Refreshment. He should remember, too, that his Jewel of Office is the Cornucopia, the emblem of plenty, embraced by the open Compasses, the symbol of restraint.

CHAPTER X

THE INNER GUARD

IN Lodges under the English Constitution the Office of Inner Guard was apparently unknown until the early part of the nineteenth century. The first mention of this Officer in the *Constitutions* appeared in 1815, and the earliest known reference to his appointment is to be found in the Minutes of the Burlington Lodge, now No. 96, dated 14th December 1814.

At one time the Inner Guard was frequently distinguished by the Trowel as his emblem of Office; it was not until 1819 that the Crossed Swords were assigned to him in the *Constitutions*. No change has since been made, and to-day Brother Inner Guard is informed, when being invested with his Collar of Office by the Worshipful Master, that his Jewel is 'two swords in saltire.' His place is 'within the entrance of the Lodge' and his duties are as important as those of any other Officer; no more and no less.

It is to be regretted that some young Masons display a tendency to treat their appointment to the Office of Inner Guard somewhat lightly, as though the duties appertaining thereto were of a nature so simple as to require but a minimum of preparation and little serious consideration. Reasonable confidence in the undertaking of any Office is to be commended; over-confidence, on the other hand, frequently leads to bungling, confusion, and consequent disaster.

An illustration of the degree of perfection with which it is possible to carry out the apparently simple duties of Inner Guard was indelibly impressed on the mind of the present writer at the Festival Meeting of the Emulation Lodge of Improvement, held in the Grand Temple at Freemasons' Hall in February 1919, upon which occasion the station within the entrance of the Lodge was occupied by an experienced Past Master, a member of the Grand Stewards' Lodge,* who discharged the duties of his Office with a degree of impressive dignity and stately command which, in all probability, has rarely been equalled and never excelled at any similar demonstration or elsewhere.

Brother Inner Guard is the link of communication between the Lodge itself and the outer world, and under no circumstances should he leave his post within the entrance of the Lodge. He is in charge of the door of the Lodge and nothing must induce him to lose control of the door while it is open; no Brother, however distinguished in rank, should be permitted to pass *between* the Inner Guard and the door. If the Inner Guard will make a practice of

* W. Bro. G. K. B. Neal, P.G.Stwd.

keeping hold of the door each time he opens it, then none can pass between him and his charge.

In a well-arranged Temple or Lodge Room the door should be in the West or quasi-West. There are many Lodge Rooms where this convenient arrangement is not to be found, but, whatever may be the location of the door, the correct position for the Inner Guard's chair is *at the immediate left of the S.W.'s pedestal.* All reports should be given from that position, *and from no other.*

A report on the door by the Tyler is the signal (if no business be in progress) for the Inner Guard to rise, take Sp., show Sn. of the Degree, and inform the Junior Warden that 'there is a report.'* Upon receiving the J.W.'s answer in the usual manner Brother Inner Guard discharges Sn. and goes to the door. Having received the Tyler's announcement he closes the door, *not forgetting to lock it,* returns to position *in front of his chair,* and repeats the Tyler's report to the Master. In each case the Inner Guard must remember not to discharge his Sn. until he has been answered by the Master or Junior Warden.

When the Tyler gives a report on the door of the Lodge the Inner Guard should remember that he *never* reports direct to the Master, but *always* to the Junior Warden. The J.W. will reply by ——▌,

* In all cases, when reporting to the J.W., the I.G. should remember not to turn his *body* towards the S. The I.G. should stand square to the E., turning *only his head* towards the J.W. when he addresses him.

or, in the case of a Candidate awaiting admission, he will first report to the W.M., and will then give the I.G. verbal instructions. After opening the door and receiving the Tyler's report, the I.G. then reports direct to the W.M. *in every case.*

When admitting either a Member or Visitor the I.G. should inform him in what Degree the Lodge is working, in order that the correct salute may be given. No Brother, however elevated in rank, should be admitted to the Lodge until he has been duly reported to the Master. The Inner Guard who is never called upon to exercise his authority in this connection may count himself fortunate; it is noticeable that Brother Secretary (who should certainly know better!) frequently appears to consider himself vested with the right to slip in and out of the Lodge in an informal manner. The Inner Guard who resolutely declines to permit such irregularity may possibly earn the momentary displeasure of an impatient Brother Secretary, but he should allow no such thought to deter him in the proper execution of his responsible duties.

Brother Inner Guard should remember that Brethren do not 'demand' admission; they 'seek' or 'request.' * According to the Emulation system

* The only Brethren in Metropolitan Masonry with power to 'demand' admission to the Lodge are the M.W. Grand Master, the M.W. Pro Grand Master, and the R.W. Deputy Grand Master. In Provinces and Districts, the R.W. Provincial or District Grand Master, and their Deputy or Assistant Provincial or District Grand Masters. No other Brother has any such right, unless acting as the directly

neither word is used; the formula is: 'W.M., Bro. A.B.,' whereupon the W.M. answers: 'Admit him.'

In only one instance does the Inner Guard ever address the J.W. *by name*, *i.e.* when the Lodge is being opened in the First Degree. The J.W. will direct the I.G. *by name* to see t.t.L.i.p.t. Having done so the I.G. reports to the J.W. *by name* that t.L.i.p.t. In the instance referred to there is no Sp. or Sn. In every other case the I.G. takes Sp., shows Sn., and addresses his Senior Officer in the South as 'Brother Junior Warden.' The Master is *never* addressed by name.

Brother Inner Guard must be careful to remember that in the First Degree *only* a Candidate is described as '*Mr*' when he is announced. In the Second and Third Degrees he is '*Brother*.' The Inner Guard should never open the door to admit a Candidate for any Degree until the Deacon responsible for that duty has placed the K.S.* in position,

accredited representative of the Grand Master. There is a widespread impression in many directions that a Grand Lodge Officer is empowered to 'demand' admission, but it is erroneous. No Grand Officer, however high in rank (save those already mentioned), has any greater claim to enter a Lodge than the youngest Master Mason; the Master has a right to refuse admission (see Chapter XXVI, p. 221, para. 10). Nor, it may be noted, is a Grand Officer visiting the Lodge vested with the slightest authority, by virtue of his rank, to interfere in any way with the proceedings or question the Master's control of affairs. If his advice is sought, doubtless he will gladly give it; if not, then the only thing which distinguishes him from other visiting Brethren is the colour of his regalia.

* See footnote, p. 138.

nor until *both* Deacons are ready at the door to receive the Candidate.

When directed by the W.M. to admit a Candidate the I.G. must always remember to take with him to the door the P.n...d, Sq., or C.'s, according to the Degree. In the First Degree, after use of the P.n...d the I.G. should hold it aloft to intimate to the W.M. that it has been so used, and then replace it on the S.W.'s ped., where the S.D. may find it at the proper time.*

The I.G. is often uncertain as to the correct method of applying the P.n...d, Sq., or C.'s. In the First Degree the p...t of the P.n...d should be applied to Can.'s n.l.b. In the Second Degree the arms of the Sq. should be applied. In Third Degree the extended p...ts of the C.'s simultaneously to Can.'s b.'s.

* It is the duty of the S.D., and *not* of the I.G., to take the P.n...d to the W.M. The latter practice is a common one and is sometimes upheld by the statement that the P.n...d is the I.G.'s particular Working Tool or Emblem, a line of reasoning difficult to follow when it is remembered that the use of the P.n...d in the First Degree is duplicated exactly by the use of the Sq. or C.'s in the Second and Third Degrees. The I.G.'s Emblem or Jewel of Office, as he is informed by the W.M. upon investiture, is 'two swords in saltire.' There is but one armed Officer of the Lodge, the Tyler who guards the porch with a d..wn s...d. The P.n...d is not a weapon either of offence or defence, it is no more than an implement used for a certain purpose in the First Degree, as are the Sq. and C.'s in the Second and Third Degrees, and it is in no sense the peculiar badge, emblem, or tool of the I.G. The I.G. should not leave his post within the entrance of the Lodge ; but the S.D., as the W.M.'s particular messenger, is correct in carrying the P.n...d with him to the E., and placing it on the W.M.'s ped. ready for use at a later stage of the Ceremony. (See also para. 2, p. 154, under " The Senior Deacon.")

When receiving a Candidate the I.G. should *never go outside the Lodge*; his position is *within the entrance of the Lodge*, and the Tyler should conduct the Candidate to such a position that the P.n...d, Sq., or C.'s may be correctly applied while the I.G. is standing *just within the entrance of the Lodge*.

Perhaps it is expecting rather much of Brother Inner Guard, who is frequently a young and inexperienced Mason, to rely upon him to see that Visiting Brethren are correctly clothed and wearing no extraneous jewels; but he should have a watchful eye for such details. In like manner he should be on the alert to see that Brother Tyler has made no blunder in a certain important part of his duties, *i.e.* that the Candidate is P.P.

No important ceremonial work should ever be interrupted for the purpose of making a report; reports given by the Tyler at inconvenient periods should be ignored. If in doubt as to whether to pay heed to a report, the Inner Guard may try to attract the attention of the J.W.; if no sign be forthcoming from that quarter, he may perhaps be able to catch the eye of the W.M. or I.P.M., receiving from that direction a silent indication as to whether to announce the report or await a more convenient moment.

Brother Inner Guard should study the following notes which will be of assistance to him in the discharge of his duties.

OPENING THE LODGE

1.—The I.G. should *show no Sn.* when directed by the J.W. to see t.t.L.i.p.t. The I.G. proceeds to the door and gives K.'s of the *First Degree. He should not open the door.* * The Tyler will answer with similar K.'s. The I.G. then returns to position *in front of his chair* and reports to the J.W. *by name*: 'Bro. . . ., t.L.i.p.t.' At this stage there should be no Sp. or Sn.

2.—When the W.M. has declared the Lodge 'duly open' and the wardens have given ➜, the I.G. again proceeds to the door and gives K.'s of the *First Degree*, which will be duly answered by the Tyler.

OPENING THE LODGE IN THE SECOND DEGREE

3.—The I.G. *shows no Sn.* when directed by the J.W. to see that t.L.i.p.t. He proceeds to the door and gives K.'s of the *First Degree*, which will be answered by the Tyler. I.G. then returns to position, takes Sp., shows Sn. of E.A., and reports: 'Bro. J.W., the L.i.p.t.' Dis. Sn. after report, keeping the hand *open*.

4.—When the W.M. has declared the Lodge

* This direction applies in the Openings in all Degrees. The J.W.'s command to the I.G. to 'see' that t.L.i.p.t. is not intended to mean that the I.G. must actually open the door. The word 'see' has other meanings than 'to perceive by the eye.' The answering K.'s from without are sufficient indication that the Tyler is at his post and that the Lodge *is* p.t.

'duly open on the Sq.' and the Wardens have given —✠, the I.G. again proceeds to the door and gives K.'s of the *Second Degree*, which will be answered by the Tyler.

OPENING THE LODGE IN THE THIRD DEGREE

5.—The I.G. *shows no Sn.* when directed by the J.W. to see t.t.L.i.p.t. He proceeds to the door and gives the K.'s of the *Second Degree*, which will be answered by the Tyler. I.G. then returns to position, takes Sp., shows Sn. of F.C., and reports: 'Bro. J.W., t.L.i.p.t.' Dis. Sn. after report, keeping *both hands open*.

6.—When the W.M. has declared the Lodge 'duly open on the C.' and the Wardens have given —✠, the I.G. again proceeds to the door and gives K.'s of the *Third Degree*, which will be answered by the Tyler.

CLOSING THE LODGE IN THE THIRD DEGREE

7.—The I.G. *shows no Sn.* when directed by the J.W. to 'prove t.L.c.t.' He proceeds to the door and gives the K.'s of the *Third Degree*, which will be answered by the Tyler. I.G. then returns to position, takes Sp., shows P.Sn. of a M.M., and reports: 'Bro. J.W., t.L.i.c.t.' Dis. Sn. after report, keeping the hand *open*, and *not forgetting to recover*.

8.—When the J.W. has declared that the Lodge

is 'closed accordingly' and given ━┫, the I.G. again proceeds to the door and gives K.'s of the *Third Degree*, which will be answered by the Tyler.

CLOSING THE LODGE IN THE SECOND DEGREE

9.—The I.G. *shows no Sn.* when directed by the J.W. to 'prove t.L.c.t.' He proceeds to the door and gives the K.'s of the *Second Degree*, which will be answered by the Tyler. I.G. then returns to position, takes Sp., shows Sn. of F.C., and reports: 'Bro. J.W., t.L.i.c.t.' Dis. Sn. after report, keeping *both hands open.*

10.—When J.W. has given ━┫ after 'And Happy Meet Again,' the I.G. again proceeds to the door and gives K.'s of the *Second Degree*, which will be answered by the Tyler.

CLOSING THE LODGE GENERALLY

11.—The I.G. *shows no Sn.* when directed by the J.W. to 'prove t.L.c.t.' He proceeds to the door and gives the K.'s of the *First Degree*, which will be answered by the Tyler. I.G. then returns to position, takes Sp., shows Sn. of E.A. and reports: 'Bro. J.W., t.L.i.c.t.' Dis. Sn. after report, keeping the hand *open.*

12.—When the J.W. has declared that the Lodge is 'closed accordingly' and given ━┫, the I.G. again proceeds to the door and gives K.'s of the *First Degree*, which will be answered by the Tyler.

THE CEREMONY OF INITIATION

1.—When the Tyler gives report for the Can. the I.G. should rise, take Sp., show Sn. of E.A., and announce to the J.W.: 'Bro. J.W., t.i.a.r.' I.G. must *remain standing to O.* while J.W. reports to the W.M. Upon receiving J.W.'s instructions the I.G. should dis. Sn., keeping the hand *open.* He then proceeds to the door, opens it, and demands of the Tyler: 'Whom h.y.t.?'

2.—After bidding Tyler to 'Halt, while I report . . . .,' the I.G. should close the door, *not forgetting to lock it,* return to position *in front of his chair,* take Sp., show Sn. of E.A., and repeat T.'s report to the W.M.

3.—When asked by the W.M. whether he vouches that the Can. is p.p. the I.G. answers: 'I do, W.M.' The I.G. should *not bow* to the W.M. when making this reply.

4.—The correct moment for the I.G. to dis. Sn. is when the W.M. speaks the words, '. . . in due form.'

5.—The I.G. takes p.n...d and proceeds to the door. He must not open it until *both* Deacons are ready to receive the Candidate. I.G. applies p.n...d and asks Can.: 'Do y.f.a.?' He then holds p.n...d aloft so that the W.M. may see it. The I.G. should place the p.n...d on S.W.'s ped. after use.*

6.—When the Tyler gives next report for the Can. who is waiting to be readmitted for the Charge the I.G. rises, takes Sp., shows Sn. of E.A., and announces to the J.W.: 'Bro. J.W., t.i.a.r.' I.G.

* See footnote on p. 101.

should not dis. Sn. until the J.W. has answered by
——🔨. I.G. then proceeds to the door to receive
Tyler's announcement, after which he closes the
door, *not forgetting to lock it*, returns to position *in
front of his chair*, takes Sp., shows Sn. of E.A., and
reports: 'W.M., the Can. on his return.' Dis. Sn.
when W.M. has replied. I.G. then again proceeds
to the door, but he should not open it until the J.D.
is ready to receive the Can.

THE CEREMONY OF PASSING

1.—When the Tyler gives the report for the Can.
the I.G. should rise, take Sp., show Sn. of F.C., and
announce to the J.W.: 'Bro. J.W., t.i.a.r.' I.G.
must *remain standing to O.* while J.W. reports to the
W.M. Upon receiving J.W.'s instructions the I.G.
should dis. Sn., keeping *both hands open*. He then
proceeds to the door, opens it, and demands of the
Tyler: 'Whom h.y.t.?' *

2.—After bidding Tyler to 'Halt,' the I.G. proceeds as in First Degree, returns to position, takes
Sp., shows Sn. of F.C., and repeats report to W.M.

3.—Again the I.G. should remember *not* to bow
to the W.M. when answering: 'I do, W.M.' †

4.—The correct moment for the I.G. to dis. Sn.

* In each Degree the I.G. must remember that he should
not actually *leave the Lodge* for his examination of the Can.
He should be standing *just within the entrance of the Lodge*
(see p. 102).

† Ceremonial bowing to the W.M. on the part of any Officer
is quite superfluous and out of place. Due respect to the
Chair is shown by the salute. Nothing further is necessary.

is when the W.M. speaks the words: '. . . in due form.'

5.—The I.G. now takes the Sq., and proceeds to the door, waiting until *both* Deacons are ready before he opens it. He applies Sq. and holds it aloft so that the W.M. may see it. (NOTE.—See p. 101 for correct method of applying the Sq.)

6.—When the Tyler gives report for the Can. who is waiting to be readmitted for Explanation of the T.B. the I.G. rises, takes Sp., shows Sn. of F.C., and announces to the J.W.: 'Bro. J.W., t.i.a.r.' I.G. should not dis. Sn. until J.W. has answered by ▬🔨. I.G. then proceeds to the door to receive Tyler's announcement, after which he closes the door, *not forgetting to lock it*, returns to position *in front of his chair*, takes Sp., shows Sn. of F.C., and reports: 'W.M., the Can. on his return.' Dis. Sn. when W.M. has replied. I.G. then again proceeds to the door, but he should not open it until the S.D. is ready to receive the Can.

THE CEREMONY OF RAISING

1.—When the Tyler gives report for the Can. the I.G. should rise, take Sp., show P.Sn. of a M.M., and announce to the J.W.: 'Bro. J.W., t.i.a.r.' I.G. must *remain standing to O.* while the J.W. reports to the W.M. Upon receiving the J.W.'s instructions the I.G. should dis. Sn., keeping the hand *open*, and *not forgetting to recover*. He then proceeds to the door, opens it, and demands of the Tyler: 'Whom h.y.t.?'

2.—After bidding Tyler to 'Halt' the I.G. proceeds as in First and Second Degrees, returns to position, takes Sp., shows P.Sn. of a M.M., and repeats report to the W.M.

3.—The correct moment for the I.G. to dis. Sn. is when the W.M. says the words: '. . . in due form.'

4.—The I.G. now takes the C.'s and proceeds to the door, waiting until *both* Deacons are ready before he opens it. He applies the C.'s, and holds them aloft so that the W.M. may see them. (NOTE.—See p. 101 for correct method of applying the C.'s.)

5.—When the Tyler gives report for the Can. who is waiting to be readmitted for completion of the Ceremony the I.G. rises, takes Sp., shows P.Sn. of a M.M., and announces to the J. W.: 'Bro. J.W., t.i.a.r.' I.G. should not dis. Sn. until J.W. has replied by ——. I.G. then proceeds to the door to receive Tyler's announcement, after which he closes the door, *not forgetting to lock it*, returns to position *in front of his chair*, takes Sp., shows Sn. of M.M., and reports: 'W.M., the Can. on his return.' Dis. Sn. when W.M. has replied. I.G. then again proceeds to the door, but he should not open it until the S.D. is ready to receive the Can.

Finally, Brother Inner Guard, pay close attention to the Tyler when he announces to you a Visiting Brother who is seeking admission. Amazing and amusing blunders are frequently heard from nervous Inner Guards when announcing the rank of a visitor. In any case of doubt do not be afraid to ask Brother

Tyler to repeat his announcement. Never hurry about your duties; remember that your work is of equal importance to that of your senior Officers. Give your reports slowly and distinctly, maintain an erect attitude and a confident demeanour, and you will do your share towards preserving that dignity and decorum which should characterise all our proceedings.

CHAPTER XI

THE ASSISTANT SECRETARY

BROTHER ASSISTANT SECRETARY is the sixth on the list of *permissive* Officers, *i.e.* those Officers who, in accordance with Rule 129 in the *Constitutions*, *may* be appointed if the Worshipful Master so desires. In Lodges where such an appointment is made the Assistant Secretary ranks immediately above the Inner Guard. His Jewel of Office is 'two pens in saltire surmounted by a bar bearing the word *Assistant*.'

As is denoted by the name of his Office, Brother Assistant Secretary's duty is to act as helper to his Senior Officer in the North. That help may be rendered in a variety of ways, but so much depends upon the personality of Brother Secretary, as well as upon Lodge customs, that no useful purpose would here be served by endeavouring to set out in detail the duties of an Assistant Secretary.

In some Lodges the Office is made a progressive one,* being regarded as the next step in promotion

---

* Strictly speaking, no Office can be regarded as '*progressive*' in the sense that the Officer has any *right* or *claim* to progress therefrom to higher Office the following year. Rule 129,

after the Office of Inner Guard. Where such a custom obtains the young Mason invested with the Collar of Assistant Secretary will, in all probability, find his Office to be in the nature of a sinecure. Lack of knowledge and experience make it impossible for him to render useful assistance in any matters of importance, and few Lodge Secretaries have either the time or the inclination to teach a fresh Assistant each year.

In other Lodges the practice is adopted of appointing the same Assistant Secretary year after year. In such cases the Brother selected by succeeding Masters is usually a trustworthy Past Master, and here valuable assistance *can* be rendered *if* Brother Secretary will accept it. The doubt implied by the italics is not an imaginary one because, strangely enough, there *are* some Lodge Secretaries who seem to *resent* the appointment of an Assistant Secretary, apparently regarding such an appointment as a reflection on their own abilities.

Where such a state of affairs exists Worshipful Brother Assistant Secretary will probably resign himself to the prospect of wearing his Collar of Office in enforced idleness; but, where happier conditions obtain, he can become a very real helper to his Senior Officer and an asset to his Lodge.

With the enormous and continued growth in the

B. of C., emphasises that no Brother has ' the right to claim advancement by rotation.' The appointment of all Officers, except the Treasurer and Tyler, is in the sole discretion and power of the Master.

size of many Lodges the work at the Secretary's table has increased proportionately. The sole responsibility for the proper discharge of that work must, of course, rest with Brother Secretary himself; but, where he accepts the willing aid of an efficient Assistant, he will find his labours considerably lightened and there will be little likelihood of the secretarial work of the Lodge falling into arrears.

CHAPTER XII

THE ORGANIST

THE Office of Brother Organist is one which, as stated in Rule 129 of the *Constitutions*, 'may' be filled if the Worshipful Master so decides.

Whether it *should* be filled is dependent upon the talent available. Certainly a Master will be wise who leaves the Office vacant rather than appoint a Brother lacking in musical ability. Unfortunately such appointments are frequently made, but the Brother who accepts the Lyre as his Emblem of Office without possessing the qualifications essential to enable him to discharge the duties of that Office in an efficient manner is something more than a source of embarrassment to his Lodge; he is a nuisance.

In cases where no Brother skilled in the divine art of Music is to be found among the members of the Lodge, and where financial or other considerations prohibit the engagement of a paid musician, the Master will be well advised to remember that music is no essential part of Masonry and that our ceremonies need lose nothing of their solemn beauty although music be entirely absent from the proceedings.

Assuming that an expert musical Brother is available, his duties are such as cannot be set out in detail within the space of a few paragraphs. The accompaniment of the Opening and Closing Odes, and of the chanting of the responses to the Prayers, are obvious duties. All else must be dependent to a great extent upon the customs existing in any particular Lodge.

However accomplished a musician the Organist may be, he must study the Ritual of the various Ceremonies closely if his efforts are to be effective. The newly appointed Organist who is young in the Craft will do well to limit his activities to the points above mentioned, and not to attempt incidental music during the Ceremonies. Later, as he gains experience and confidence, he will be able to make musical interpolations with advantage.

No disrespect to Brother Organist is intended if he is here reminded that he had better be heard too seldom than too frequently; the organ should *never* be permitted to obtrude unduly on the Ceremony. The greatest care is necessary in the interpolation of musical phrases; they must be carefully timed, and terminate precisely at the right moment.

The selection of suitable music for incidental phrases during the Ceremonies may safely be left to the discretion of an experienced musician who is also possessed of a sense of Masonic fitness. There are, however, two important points to which the attention of Brother Organist may be directed.

The first is during the Ceremony of Initiation when, after the Ob., the Candidate is about to be restored to L...t.   At this solemn moment when the Brethren, at a given signal from the W.M., make a certain movement, a loud chord from the organ is often heard.   Such a proceeding can only be termed undignified and quite out of place.

Even more undesirable is the interposition of light secular music following the investiture of the different Officers at the Installation Meeting. During these proceedings the present writer has heard the air of 'For He's a Jolly Good Fellow' coming from the organ at the investing of the Secretary, and the strains of 'Poor Old Joe' greeting the reappointment of the Tyler.

It has to be admitted that even Organists of considerable experience sometimes err in this direction. The Worshipful Master will be acting wisely if he gently but firmly intimates that such musical interpolations are undesirable and out of place.

CHAPTER XIII

THE ALMONER

BROTHER ALMONER'S Office is one of modern origin; no mention of it is to be found in the *Constitutions* until the year 1910. His jewel is 'a scrip purse upon which is a heart.' In the table of precedence the Almoner ranks between the Assistant Director of Ceremonies and the Organist.

During the impressive ceremony of Initiation we are reminded that we have ranged under our banners Brethren who are reduced to the lowest ebb of poverty and distress. To bring relief to such distressed Brethren is the duty of Brother Almoner, and to supplement the funds for this worthy cause it is the custom in most Lodges for the Almoner to circulate the Charity Box among the Brethren. Whether this should be done in Open Lodge or deferred until the period of Refreshment is a question upon which there exists a divergence of opinion. The question is one which must be left to individual Masters, who will doubtless be guided by the practice existing in their respective Lodges.

The question as to whether visiting Brethren should be asked *or allowed* to contribute to the

Charity Box is another upon which varying opinions are held. It is scarcely to be expected that in any Lodge the Charity Box would be unduly obtruded upon a guest, but there can be no harm in *allowing* a Visiting Brother to contribute his mite to such an excellent cause if he so desires. When the present writer is asked by a Brother who is about to take round the Charity Box whether it is to be taken to the Visitors he invariably answers: "Pass them *slowly*."

In many Lodges the custom exists of making the Almoner's Office a progressive * one, the Brother who has filled the Office of Inner Guard (or perhaps Assistant Secretary) one year acting as Almoner the next. There is much to be said against such a practice; it is highly improbable that the junior Mason, who has some five or six years to wait before he attains the rank of an Installed Master, can possess the necessary experience to qualify him to discharge the duties of the Almoner's Office in an efficient manner.

Frequently, when application is made for relief, considerable experience is *essential* to enable Brother Almoner to decide whether the case is one worthy of support, for it is unhappily true that we have in our midst Masonic vagrants who seek to trade upon their connection with the Order by imposing upon the charitable instincts of the Brethren.

The Almoner who is reappointed year after year,

* See footnote on p. 111 under " Assistant Secretary."

and who thus becomes as *permanent* an Officer of
the Lodge as the Treasurer and Secretary,* accumu-
lates a store of experience which cannot fail to be
of advantage to him in the execution of his duties.
From all points of view Brother Almoner should be
a *permanent* Officer of the Lodge and a Past Master
of experience.

* In a literal sense there are, of course, no ' permanent '
Officers of a Lodge, each Officer being appointed (or elected)
each year.   Nevertheless it is the custom in many Lodges for
such Officers as the Treasurer, Secretary, D.C., Organist, etc.,
to hold their Offices for long periods, so that they become in
practice, if not in theory, more or less ' permanent ' officials.

CHAPTER XIV

THE ASSISTANT DIRECTOR OF CEREMONIES

RULE 18, *Book of Constitutions*, states that the Grand Master shall appoint two *Deputy* Grand Directors of Ceremonies and twelve *Assistant* Grand Directors of Ceremonies. It should be noted that there is a wide difference between the two Offices. The '*Deputy*,' as his designation denotes, is one appointed to act in the place of his Senior Officer when occasion demands, whereas the '*Assistant*' is an auxiliary Officer whose duty it is to render such *assistance* as may be required of him.

It would appear, therefore, that in a Private Lodge our Brother the Assistant Director of Ceremonies would be more correctly designated as 'Deputy' since, as a general rule, he is expected to *deputise* in the absence of the Director of Ceremonies.

As in the case of the Almoner and Assistant Secretary, the Office of Assistant Director of Ceremonies is in many Lodges made a progressive * one, the Brother acting in that capacity one year progressing to the Office of Junior Deacon the following year, always provided that the Master is pleased to promote him.

* See footnote on p. 111 under " Assistant Secretary."

There is much to be said against the practice and little in its favour. The younger Brother who is working his way upward through the various Offices cannot be expected to possess the wide experience which is essential for the efficient discharge of the manifold duties of a Director of Ceremonies, and he is consequently unfitted to act in that capacity in the absence of his Senior Officer. On Installation nights, for instance, he would be compelled to be absent from the Lodge during the most important part of the proceedings.

Undoubtedly the Assistant Director of Ceremonies should be a Past Master and, where the right Brother has been found for the Office, the newly installed Master will be wise to confirm the choice of his predecessor by reappointing the previous holder of the Office.

To attempt to set out in detail the duties of the Assistant Director of Ceremonies would necessitate a recapitulation of the points dealt with in Chapter XVIII, for the efficient Assistant should be in every way as expert in the mysteries of the Craft as his Senior Officer. As already mentioned, it is his duty to deputise in the absence of the Director of Ceremonies, and he can only discharge such a responsible duty in a proper manner if he be thoroughly conversant with Masonic etiquette and the conducting of our ceremonial proceedings. Brother Assistant Director of Ceremonies should read Chapter XVIII carefully, and master the hints therein contained.

Where the Junior Officer is acting in his capacity of *Assistant* it is essential that he should arrive at a perfect understanding with his senior Brother and that he should know exactly what is expected of him. However distinguished a Past Master he may be, the Assistant Director of Ceremonies should ever be on his guard not to allow any excess of zeal to influence him to 'jump in' and take upon himself any duty rightly belonging to the Director of Ceremonies. Any such action, however well intended, would be likely to lead to regrettable friction.

On the other hand, where perfect understanding and fraternal goodwill exist between the Director of Ceremonies and his Assistant the ceremonial portion of our solemn proceedings will certainly be conducted with imposing dignity and decorum, and Profit and Pleasure will be the happy result.*

* See footnote, p. 163, as to A.D.C.'s station in the Lodge.

CHAPTER XV

THE DEACONS

IT would be difficult in these days even for the most imaginative Brother to conceive a mental picture of our Craft Ceremonies being carried through without the assistance of those of our Brethren who are distinguished by the familiar emblem of a Dove bearing a Branch of Olive, the symbol of Peace and Knowledge.

Yet the general adoption of the Office of Deacon, as we know it to-day, is of fairly modern origin in private Lodges working under the jurisdiction of the United Grand Lodge of England. In the early Scotch and Irish Lodges Deacons were important officials, and in the ancient records of a few private English Lodges references to Deacons are to be found as far back as the early part of the eighteenth century; but these useful Officers were not commonly known in English Lodges working under the Regular Grand Lodge until some eighty years later.

It was on 13th December 1809 that the Brethren of the Lodge of Promulgation resolved that:

"Deacons being proved on due investigation to be not only ancient but useful and necessary Officers, be recommended."

The fact that, prior to that time, Brother Deacon had not been considered a necessary Officer in the majority of English Lodges suggests that the respective Ceremonies of Making, Passing, and Raising a Mason must have been of an extremely simple order, with very little work of a ceremonial nature.

In these modern times, as is well known, the duties of the Deacons are of the utmost importance. Indeed, if any one Office in the Lodge can be said to be of greater importance than another, it is surely that of the Deacon. It has often been said that it is the Deacons who make or mar the success of any one of our Ceremonies. There is much truth in the statement. Even though the work of the Master be imperfect, halting, and slovenly, smart and correct work by the Deacons will do much towards removing an unfavourable impression of the proceedings as a whole. On the contrary, it is equally true that, however impressive and excellent may be the work of the Master, the whole effect of the Ceremony will inevitably be ruined, should the Deacons perform their respective duties in a slipshod, hesitating manner.

It must be remembered that Brother Deacon is in the focus of the limelight practically from start to finish. He is the cynosure of all eyes, for the simple reason that he is in immediate charge of the Candidate; and the Candidate is the centre of interest and attraction. Without efficiency on the part of the

Deacons it is no exaggeration to say that our solemn and beautiful Ceremonies cannot possibly produce that desirable effect which they should always produce in the heart and mind of a Candidate in any Degree.

Every Deacon, Senior or Junior, should have a thorough knowledge of the Ritual; to be efficient and reliable in the discharge of his important duties he should be as familiar with the Ritual of the Three Degrees as the Master himself. The Deacon who is happily conversant with the Ritual will know exactly *what* to do, *how* to do it, and *when* to do it. As a result any awkward hiatus in the proceedings will thus be avoided.

In many systems of working the Deacons receive frequent prompting as to their movements from the Master, a form of procedure which can scarcely be said to add to the dignity of any solemn ceremony. In Emulation-working, the system with which we are here concerned, no such interruptions mar the smooth progress of the Ceremony. *Brother Deacon is expected to know his work.*

Assuming that the newly invested Deacon, for whom these words are written, has acquired some familiarity with the wording of the Ceremonies, he will probably proceed to make the discovery that the responsible duties of his Office are such as to demand a comprehensive knowledge of many details not to be learnt from any printed Ritual. Accurate though the printed Ritual may be in the actual phraseology of the Ceremonies, limitations of space preclude the inclusion therein of those essential directions without which the young Mason, recently invested or about to be invested with a Deacon's collar, is left in a bewildering state of uncertainty.

The following general hints and directions are offered for the guidance of newly appointed Deacons, but it is here urged upon our younger Brethren that there is one place and one place only where they can acquire the requisite knowledge to fit them for the proper discharge of the obligations of their Office. That place, needless to say, is within a regularly constituted Lodge of Instruction, presided over by a competent and trustworthy Preceptor.*

GENERAL HINTS FOR DEACONS

1.—*When giving Directions.*

The direction to the Can. to s.o.w.t.l.f. should be whispered or spoken in an undertone. Similarly the directions as to how he should place his f. for the three irreg. sps. in adv. to the W.M.'s ped. in the First Degree. Most other directions should be spoken quite distinctly.

2.—*When Prompting.*

Do not whisper or mumble. Speak clearly and audibly so that the prompts can be heard by all the Brethren and much will be done towards keeping the

* See p. 283 for list of recognised Emulation-working Lodges of Instruction.

attention of the assembly concentrated on the Ceremony.

3.—*The Deacon's Wand.*

The Deacon should remember that his wand is his '*Badge of Office.*' He should not use it as a walking-stick when perambulating the Lodge, nor as a crutch when standing still. There can scarcely be a more undignified sight in the Lodge than the Deacon who clutches his wand with both hands and leans upon it. Unfortunately such a spectacle is all too common. The wand should be held lightly and naturally at about the centre, the butt kept an inch or so from the floor when perambulating the Lodge, and resting lightly on the floor when at a halt. The Deacon should keep his wand *perpendicular*. Above all, it should be kept in the *right hand* and the Deacon cannot well go wrong. The only occasions when a Deacon need transfer his wand to his left hand are during Obs. and Prs. when the r.h. may be otherwise engaged. With a little practice all Sns. can be given without the wand being transferred to the l.h. It is not necessary for the S.D. to take his wand when fetching the Minute Book from the Secretary's table to the Master's ped. for signature; nor for the J.D. to take his wand when attending to the changing the T.B.'s; nor for either Deacon to carry his wand when attending to duties in connection with a ballot. At all other times the Deacons should carry their wands.

4.—*General Demeanour.*

Maintain a smart, soldierly bearing throughout the ceremony. Deacons can *command* the attention of the Brethren by their manner. Keep alert. Do not allow your thoughts to wander or you will miss your cues. Follow the work of the W.M. and W.'s closely.

5.—*Turning Movements with Candidate.*

Much indecision is displayed by Deacons when turning away from the W.M.'s ped., and again at the N.W. corner of the Lodge. Deacons should remember always to turn so that they *interpose themselves* between the Can. and the W.M.'s ped. The single exception to this rule is immediately after a Can. has been entrusted with the P.G. and P.W leading to a higher Degree.

6.—*Candidate's Sns.*

Never permit a Can. to give a Sn. until he has first taken the Sp. Always direct the Can. in a whisper to take the Sp. and if necessary check a premature Sn. with your l.h.

7.—*Ballots.*

When there is a ballot to be taken the J.D. goes ahead with the voting tokens, the S.D. following with the box. The J.D. should give the first token to the I.P.M., then proceed down the S., across the W., up the N., and so back to the E., giving the last token to the W.M.* The S.D. should first submit the ballot-box to the W.M. or I.P.M. for examination before proceeding to collect the tokens. It

* Such is the method followed at the Emulation Lodge of Improvement. In many regular Lodges the practice is for the J.D. to give the *first* token to the W.M.

must be quite certain that the 'Nay' drawer is *empty* before the tokens are collected.

8.—*Opening and Closing the Lodge.*

It is the duty of the *Junior* Deacon to attend to the changing of the T.B.'s.*

9.—*Minutes.*

When the W.M. has declared the Minutes confirmed it is the duty of the S.D. to fetch the Minute-Book from the Secretary's table, present it for signature, and return it to the Secretary.† S.D. should try to avoid resting the Minute-Book on the V.S.L. (NOTE.—See para. 3, p. 127, as to wand.)

Further and more detailed directions relating to the work of the Deacons are set out in the two subsequent chapters.

* During the Opening and Closing of the Lodge in any Degree the J.D. should *not* leave his place to attend to the T.B. until *after* the J.W. has given K.'s. It is to be regretted that in many of the recognised Lodges of Instruction the J.D. is taught to attend to this duty immediately the Master has given K.'s during the Openings, or the S.W. has done so during the Closings, with the result that, during the Closings, the J.D. is causing confusion by moving about the Lodge *while the J.W. is speaking*. Dignified and orderly ceremonial surely demands that the J.W. should be permitted to complete his portion of the Ceremony without such interruption. The plea that the custom referred to 'saves time' borders on the ridiculous. The time 'saved' cannot be more than two or three seconds—a poor excuse for the sacrifice of decorum.

† At the Emulation Lodge of Improvement this is not done, as the Minutes are not signed.

9

CHAPTER XVI

THE JUNIOR DEACON

THE situation of the Junior Deacon is at the right of the Senior Warden, and his duties, as explained to him on investiture, include *attendance on Candidates during the Ceremony of Initiation.* A little reflection may show that these few italicised words refer to what may perhaps be described as the most important duty in the whole gamut of Masonic Ceremonial, with the single exception of the duties of the Worshipful Master.

First impressions in Masonry, as in other spheres of life, are often indelible. It is the Junior Deacon who receives from the hands of the Inner Guard the blind, helpless seeker after Masonic light. Any suggestion of bungling, of undue nervousness, or, what would be far worse, of levity, displayed by the Junior Deacon at this solemn juncture might well destroy for all time the Candidate's favourable impressions of the beneficent Fraternity into which he is seeking admission. Gentle firmness, combined with complete self-control and proper knowledge, on the part of the Junior Deacon, may do much towards producing in the Candidate's mind a love for the Craft which may never fade with the passing of the years.

Brother Junior Deacon may well pay heed to those impressive words contained in the Second Section of the First Lecture which tell how the Candidate being '*neither naked nor clothed, barefoot nor shod, but in an humble, halting, moving posture*' was '*friendly taken by the right hand.*'

Friendly taken by the right hand. The Junior Deacon should remember that word upon which emphasis is placed and regard it as no unimportant part of his duty to constitute himself the guiding friend of the novice in his charge. It may rest very largely with the Junior Deacon whether there remains in the Candidate's mind a lasting and beautiful impression of the solemn ceremony of his entry into our Order.

Much may be done by the tactful Junior Deacon to help a Candidate even *before* the Ceremony of his Initiation. In the course of a brief, friendly chat in the anteroom the ice may be broken, as it were, and a few brotherly hints conveyed without, of course, revealing anything that should remain hidden. A very nervous Candidate tends to mar a Ceremony; some Candidates anticipate foolery, practical joking—even danger. Brother Junior Deacon may tactfully explain that the Ceremony about to take place is of a serious and solemn nature and that there is no cause for fear.

The annexed guiding hints in connection with the

Initiation and subsequent Ceremonies should be carefully studied by the Junior Deacon.

THE CEREMONY OF INITIATION

1.—In this Degree, during the actual Ceremony, the seniority of the Deacons may be said to be reversed; it is the *Junior* Deacon who is in control of the Candidate, the S.D. acting in the capacity of *assistant* where necessary.

2.—The W.M. having given directions for the Can.'s admission, the J.D. takes his wand in his r.h. and goes to the door. He should receive the Can. gently, but his hold should be a firm one; nothing is more likely to increase a Can.'s bewilderment and nervousness than being controlled in a limp, hesitating manner. The best method of controlling a Can., particularly in the early stages of the Initiation Ceremony, is for the Deacon to see that his l.a. is *behind* the Can.'s r.a. J.D. leads Can. slowly to the K.S.

3.—J.D. should prompt the response to the W.M.'s first question in a low, clear voice. If hesitation is shown by Can. after W.M.'s first direction J.D. should whisper to Can. that the K.S. is before him. J.D. transfers wand to l.h., elevates it,* and places r.h. in correct attitude for Pr. The *Candidate's* r.h. is *not* so placed in this Degree. While the Can. is h.-w. the J.D. should never release his hand except during the Ob. and Pr.

* When elevated the Deacons' wands should always be crossed symmetrically and just touching.

4.—After the Pr. and subsequent question the J.D. assists Can. to rise and awaits W.M.'s proclamation before the perambulation. *Square each corner of the Lodge carefully*, whispering to Can. at start of each movement to s.o.w.t.l.f. At the Wardens' stations the signals on their s......rs should be given firmly, but *not heavily*.

5.—After the perambulation the J.D. places Can.'s r.h. in S.W.'s l.h. See that Can. is facing the E. and take place in line on his left. The Deacon should never be hidden behind the Can. J.D. should be alert to take charge of Can. again at the proper moment, and stand facing E. while receiving the S.W.'s directions. *No Sn. when addressed by S.W.*

6.—J.D. leads Can. *diagonally* (no squaring) to correct position for the three irreg. sps. About a yard from the W.M.'s ped. is sufficient. Give directions clearly, retaining firm grip, thus practically *compelling* obedience. The J.D. should *not* use his wand here to touch Can.'s f..t.

7.—Before commencement of Ob. the J.D. transfers wand to his l.h., elevates it,* takes Sp., and shows P.Sn. of an E.A. The correct moment to dis. Sn. is immediately the Can. has repeated the final words of the Ob. The J.D. should remember that when the Can. is asked by the W.M. if he is willing to take the S.Ob. his answer should be voluntary; he should *not* be prompted to say "I am."†

* See footnote, p. 132.

† If Can. hesitates the Deacon should whisper to him to answer, but on no account should the Deacon immediately say "Answer" audibly. The word is no part of the Ritual and any such practice is contrary to correct Emulation-working.

8.—The restoration to L...t is of the utmost importance. The J.D. is frequently too late or too early in discharging a certain duty; proper understanding between the W.M. and J.D. is essential if an effective impression is to be obtained. J.D. should catch W.M.'s eye to indicate that he is ready, removing h.-w. at exact moment of W.M.'s final movement with ━▌.* If the Can. remains still with eyes directed to V.S.L. there is *no need for J.D. to touch his h..d.*

9.—The W.M. having completed certain duties now following, the J.D. should place the Can. at N. side of the ped. Do not be too late or too early in removing the c.-t. The correct moment is as W.M. says the words, '. . . and done his duty.' During the entrusting the J.D. should be ready to assist if necessary, but he should not interfere unduly.† J.D. should *not* give the Sn. when W.M. does so. J.D. must be quick with prompt in response to W.M.'s third question or the Can. may answer voluntarily *and incorrectly.* When the W.M. gives the W. the J.D. repeats it to the Can., who must repeat it after him. Similar repetition by J.D. and Can. when the W.M. spells the W.

10.—After the entrusting the Lodge should be carefully *squared* when J.D. conducts Can. to the Wardens' stations. J.D. must remember to take Sp. and show Sn. before speaking at J.W.'s station.

* See para. 5, p. 242.
† At this stage and at similar stage in Second Degree the Can. should be under the sole direction of the W.M. The Deacon should not interfere unless absolutely necessary.

Similarly at S.W.'s station. Do *not* transfer wand to l.h. to give the Sn. If the butt of the wand is pushed slightly forward and the tip allowed to rest against the right shoulder the Sns. of all degrees can be given without transferring wand to the l.h. (see para. 3, p. 127). Dis. Sn. before J.W. replies. Similarly at S.W.'s station.* During examination at S.W.'s station J.D. must remember that Can. does *not* give the Sn. when directed to advance. Direct him in a whisper, checking any premature Sn. if necessary by placing l.h. on Can.'s r. w...t.

11. It is the S.W.'s duty to invest the Can. with the distinguishing badge of a M., but the J.D. should be ready to assist if necessary. At conclusion of S.W.'s remarks J.D. should turn Can. to face the E. and stand in line on his right. After W.M.'s address respecting the badge the J.D. awaits instructions to proceed. J.D. must be careful not to forget necessary instructions to the Can. at the N.E. corner. The correct position at the N.E. corner is just in line with the front of W.M.'s ped.

12.—At the N.E. corner the J.D. should *not* leave the Can. standing alone while he goes to look for the alms-dish; if it is not forthcoming it is sufficient for the J.D. to extend his l.h. when putting the first question to Can. J.D. should lower the alms-dish (or his hand) after Can. has signified that

* When the Can. communicates the G. or T. at the Wardens' stations in this and subsequent Degrees the Deacon should adjust it with his l.h. *over* the Can.'s r.a., the Deacon retaining his wand in his r.h.

he has nothing to give. J.D. should remember that the Can. is frequently confused when asked if he has 'anything to give in the cause . . .' If Can. does not answer the J.D. should proceed at once with the second question.* J.D. should stand directly in front of the W.M.'s ped., taking Sp. and showing Sn. before reporting that 'Our new-made Brother affirms . . .'

13.—The J.D. should be alert to take the Can. to the front of W.M.'s ped. at the correct moment for explanation of the W.T.'s, etc.

14.—When Can. is dismissed by the W.M. the J.D. conducts him direct to the l. of the S.W. *without squaring.*† J.D. instructs Can. to salute the W.M. as a M. Can. then retires, the J.D. escorting him to the door.‡

15.—On the Can.'s return for the Charge the J.D. meets him at the door, conducts him to l. of the S.W., and directs him to salute the W.M. as a M. The Can. should not be placed in the centre of the Lodge unless at the express direction of the W.M. The Can.'s correct position for the Charge is in the

---

* In some Lodges the practice is adopted at this point of circulating the alms-dish among the Brethren round the Lodge, the J.D. presenting it to the Can. last. Such a practice can only be regarded as an undesirable innovation with nothing to be said in its favour. There is much to be said against it. It can only add unnecessarily to the Can.'s confusion, while it creates a disturbing hiatus at a most important point in the Ceremony.

† See para. 5, p. 128.

‡ The Can. should always be permitted to leave the Lodge at this stage to restore himself to his p.c.'s. The slovenly custom of giving the Charge without allowing the Can. to retire (on the pretext of 'saving time') is one to be deprecated by all believers in orderly and dignified ceremonial.

W. at the l. of the S.W.   At the conclusion of the Charge the J.D. conducts Can. to a seat and resumes his own seat at the r. of the S.W.   The Can. should *not* be directed to salute after the Charge.

Note.—Except during the few moments when standing in front of the Can. to ask certain questions at the N.E. corner of the Lodge the J.D. should never under any circumstances leave him unattended at any time during the Ceremony.

THE CEREMONY OF PASSING

1.—The J.D. should remember that he is again in charge of the Candidate until the Lodge is actually open in the Second Degree, *i.e.* during his examination by the W.M. and while he is being entrusted with the P.G. and P.W.   After the W.M.'s announcement that 'Bro. A. B. is this evening a Candidate . . .' the J.D. conducts Can. to the W. at l. of the S.W., and stands with him facing E.*   J.D. should be ready to prompt if necessary.

2.—At conclusion of Examination J.D. conducts Can. to N. side of the W.M.'s ped. *without squaring*. J.D. repeats the P.W. after W.M., and Can. repeats it after J.D.

3.—After the entrusting J.D. conducts Can. straight to the W. at l. of the S.W. *without squaring*.†

* At Emulation Lodge of Improvement the J.D. places Can. in position *before* the W.M.'s announcement, but the method indicated in para. 1 above is the practice followed in the majority of regular Emulation-working Lodges.

† See para. 5, p. 128.

Can. is directed to salute the W.M. as a M. He then retires, the J.D. escorting him to the door.

(The Lodge is here Opened or Resumed
in the Second Degree.)

The Lodge being opened in the Second Degree the Junior Deacon immediately becomes assistant to his Brother the Senior Deacon. There is little for the Junior Deacon to do during the Ceremony of Passing, but his duties should be carried out with the same scrupulous care as those appertaining to the previous Degree. Brother Junior Deacon should pay careful attention to the following hints:—

4.—Before admission of the Can. the J.D. should place the K.S. in correct position * and proceed to the door with the S.D. After S.D. has instructed the Can. as to the method of advancing the J.D. should be careful to notice if the K.S. is in exact position for the Can. to make use of it without

* According to Emulation practice the correct position for the K.S. in the W. (when not in use) is before the S.W.'s ped., and it is the duty of the S.D. in the First Degree, and the J.D. in the Second and Third Degrees, to place it in proper position for use of the Can. during the Pr., and afterwards to replace it. This naturally implies that the K.S. is a small one which can be conveniently handled by one Officer. In some Lodges, however, more particularly in the Provinces, the K.S. is a bulky piece of furniture, sometimes fitted with a hand-rail, sufficiently heavy to need two or more Officers to move it, and too cumbersome to be kept before the S.W.'s ped. In such cases it is frequently kept in the extreme N.W. corner of the Lodge Room, or behind the S.W.'s ped., and the D.C. should see that certain Brethren are properly instructed to move it at the correct times. Deacons must, of course, adapt themselves to existing conditions.

further advancing. If it is not the J.D. should adjust it. J.D. takes position on l. of Can.

5.—During Pr. J.D. transfers wand to l.h., elevates it, and shows Sn. of R.* After Pr. J.D. should withdraw K.S.† to permit S.D. to start perambulation with Can. He then replaces the K.S. in position before S.W.'s ped. and resumes his seat.

6.—For the Ob. the J.D. should arrive at the W.M.'s ped. simultaneously with S.D. and Can. He should see that the Can.'s l.a. is correctly placed in the a...e of the Sq., and that Can.'s t...b is i.t.f.o.a.S., *pointing over his l.s.* J.D. should hold the Sq. with his r.h., transferring his wand to the l.h.‡ It is impossible here for the J.D. to show the Sn. of F., but he should remember to stand to O. by taking the Sp. After the Ob. the J.D. removes the Sq. and lowers Can.'s l.a. J.D. returns to his seat *without squaring*.

7.—On the Can.'s return to the Lodge for the Explanation of the T.B. the J.D. does *not* accompany the S.D. to the door. J.D. should wait till S.D. conducts Can. to the foot of the T.B., which should be on the floor in the centre of the Lodge; he then takes position on left of Can., and hands his wand to the W.M. for use in pointing out the emblems.

THE CEREMONY OF RAISING

1.—During this Ceremony the J.D. is again in the position of assistant to his senior colleague.

* See footnote on p. 132. † See footnote on p. 138.
‡ See para. 3, p. 127.

Immediately the Lodge is Opened or Resumed in the Third Degree the J.D. assists the S.D. to lay the S.* and ext. the L.'s.† Upon the W.M.'s direction for the admission of the Can. the J.D. should attend to the K.S.‡ as in Second Degree (see para. 4, p. 138).

2.—During the Pr. the J.D. transfers wand to his l.h., elevates it,§ and shows Sn. of R. After Pr. the J.D. should withdraw the K.S. When S.D. has started perambulation with Can. J.D. replaces K.S.‡ in position before S.W.'s ped. and follows S.D. and Can. During perambulations in this Degree the J.D. should keep place *immediately behind the Can., carefully squaring the Lodge* at each corner.

3.—After second perambulation the J.D. lines up in the W. on Can.'s left. After W.M.'s proclamation the J.D. again takes position behind Can. for third perambulation.

4.—After third perambulation, during presentation of Can. by the S.W., the J.D. takes place in line with Can. and S.D., standing on the left of his senior Officer.

5.—The J.D. again follows behind the Can. when S.D. conducts him to position for demonstration as to method of advancing to the E. J.D. takes

* Deacons should remember that the S. must be *open*. The S. should *never be folded* during any part of the ceremony.

† The Emulation Lodge of Improvement being in fact a Lodge of Instruction the L.'s are never ext. there. Therefore it seems that the Emulation Committee can lay down no exact ruling as to the point at which it should be done. Opinions vary, but the method indicated in para. 1 above is the practice followed in the great majority of regular Emulation-working Lodges.

‡ See footnote on p. 138.   § See footnote on p. 132.

place on left of Can. while S.D. demonstrates. J.D. should arrive at W.M.'s ped. simultaneously with Can. and S.D.

6.—During the Ob. the J.D. transfers wand to l.h., elevates it,* and shows P.Sn. of a M.M. Correct moment to dis. Sn. is when Can. repeats final words of the Ob. *Remember to recover.*

7.—When the Can. has been assisted by the W.M. the J.D. should step back with Can. and S.D. to foot of the C.

8.—After the Exhortation, when the W.M. summons the Wardens to assist him, the J.D. should wait until the S.W. arrives immediately behind him. He then steps aside and returns to his seat at right of the S.W.'s ped. *without squaring.*

* See footnote on p. 132.

CHAPTER XVII

THE SENIOR DEACON

BROTHER SENIOR DEACON'S situation is at *or near to* the right of the Worshipful Master. Unless expressly directed otherwise by the Master he should be careful not to interpose himself between the Chair and any Grand Lodge Officers who may be present, those distinguished Brethren having a prescriptive right to occupy the seats on the immediate right of the Master.

The Senior Deacon's Jewel of Office is exactly similar to that of his junior colleague, the Dove bearing an Olive Branch, although it may here be mentioned that the emblem of both was originally the Greek god Hermes, the herald and messenger of the gods, represented with winged cap and ankles, bearing the Caduceus adorned with wings to symbolise Speed, and entwined with a pair of serpents representing Wisdom and Health.

An ancient Lodge of which the author is a Past Master still retains the winged messenger as the Jewel of the Senior Deacon. Many old Lodges are in possession of similar jewels, but such figures, if lost or destroyed, must not be replaced with a replica. In any such case the authorities stipulate that the new jewel must be the now familiar Dove and Olive Branch.

Presuming that the newly invested Senior Deacon has passed through the earlier Offices of Inner Guard and Junior Deacon, obtaining well-merited promotion by his diligence in the discharge of the obligations attaching to those important positions, it is to be assumed that he has now gained some confidence in his own ability and knowledge, and that he is justified in looking forward to the further advancement which will bring to him the proud occupancy of the Warden's chair in the South. But the year which must elapse is one of considerable responsibility and labour for him if his Lodge is one in which the Ceremonies of Passing and Raising are to be carried out during the present Master's reign.

It is true that the Senior Deacon is not entrusted with the immediate care of the Candidate during the solemn and imposing Ceremony of Initiation, but the two subsequent Ceremonies are not of less importance. The second stage, short though it is in comparison with the others, is one full of interest; while it can scarcely be said that there is any Masonic Ceremony more sublimely beautiful and inspiring than that of Raising.

During each of these Ceremonies it is Brother Senior Deacon who is personally responsible for the conducting of the Candidate, and much will depend upon the manner in which he fills his important rôle.

The final stage will first be dealt with, and detailed directions are tabulated hereunder for the guidance of the newly invested Senior Deacon.

THE CEREMONY OF RAISING

1.—The S.D. has to remember that he is in charge of the Candidate from the start, *i.e.* before the Lodge is actually opened in the Third Degree. After the W.M.'s announcement that 'Bro. A. B. is this evening a Candidate to be . . .,' the S.D. conducts the Can. to the W., on the l. of the S.W., and stands with him facing E.* S.D. should be ready to prompt if necessary.

2.—At conclusion of Examination S.D. conducts Can. to N. side of the W.M.'s ped. *without squaring*. S.D. repeats the P.W. after the W.M., and Can. repeats it after S.D.

3.—After the Entrusting S.D. conducts Can. straight to the W. at left of the S.W. *without squaring*.† Can. is directed to salute the W.M. as a F.C., first as an E.A. He then retires, S.D. escorting him to the door.

(The Lodge is here Opened or Resumed
in the Third Degree.)

Assisted by his junior colleague the S.D. now

* At the Emulation Lodge of Improvement the S.D. places Can. in position in the W. *before* the W.M.'s announcement, but the method indicated in para. 1 above is the practice followed in the great majority of regular Emulation-working Lodges.

† See para. 5, p. 128.

attends to certain matters of preparation; he must lay the S.* and see that the L.'s are ext.†

4.—The W.M. having given directions for the Can.'s admission, the S.D. takes his wand in his r.h. and proceeds *without squaring* to the door, where he will be joined by the J.D. after the latter Officer has attended to the K.S.‡ The S.D. should be watchful to see that this duty is not forgotten. S.D. conducts Can. to within a convenient distance from the K.S., and directs him to *advance* as a F.C., first as an E.A.§ S.D. must see that the Can. takes Sp. before showing Sn. in each case.

5.—Before the Pr. the S.D. should see that the Can.'s r.h. is in correct attitude for Sn. of R. S.D. then transfers wand to his l.h., elevates it,‖ and places r.h. in correct attitude.

6.—After the Pr. S.D. assists Can. to rise and starts on the first perambulation, *squaring the Lodge carefully at each corner.* Assuming that the K.S. is one small enough to be handled conveniently by one Officer, it should be replaced in position before S.W.'s ped. by the J.D. *after* S.D. has started perambulation with Can. (see para. 2, p. 140), but the S.D. should remember to start the perambulation *very slowly*, thus giving the J.D. time to replace

* The S. should *not* be folded (see footnote on p. 140).
† See footnote on p. 140 as to correct point at which the L.'s should be ext.
‡ See footnote on p. 138.
§ Senior Deacons should note that there are only two occasions when the Can. on entering the Lodge is directed to *advance* instead of *salute*—i.e. when the Can. enters the Lodge to make *advancement* from the 1st to the 2nd Degree, or from the 2nd to the 3rd Degree.   ‖ See footnote on p. 132.

the K.S. and catch him up without noticeable hurrying. The J.D. is often seen to do something in the nature of a sprint to overtake his senior Officer and the Can. This looks undignified and should be quite unnecessary. In making the three perambulations with the Can. the S.D. should at all times remember that the J.D. should be following *immediately behind the Can.* S.D. should be particularly careful when making the turning movements at the corners of the Lodge; the movements should be made *slowly*, thus allowing the J.D. to keep in correct position without difficulty. S.D. should be careful to bring Can. to a halt at the W.M.'s ped. before directing him to salute the W.M. as a M.* The Can. should *not* turn his head or body towards the W.M. when giving the salute. Similar directions apply when Can. salutes the W.M. or Wardens at a later stage. S.D. should again bring Can. to a halt at J.W.'s station before directing him how to advance. The S.D. should *not* give the Sns. with the Can. at the Wardens' stations. (*See footnote on p.* 135 *for method of communicating the G. or T.*) After the examination by J.W. the S.D. must again be careful to bring Can. to a halt at S.W.'s ped. before directing him to salute.

7.—The second perambulation follows immedi-

---

* It is essential to halt and take Sp. before giving *any* Masonic Sn. The Sn. is one of the Ss. of the Degree. During the communication of the Ss. in each Degree it is impressed upon the Can. by the W.M. that '*it is in this position that the Ss. of the Degree are communicated.*' The *position* alluded to can be arrived at *only by taking the Sp.* Any direction to salute 'in passing' is therefore directly opposed to the Ritual.

ately after the first, the Can. again being brought to a halt at the W.M.'s and J.W.'s stations to salute as a F.C. He is then directed how to advance to the S.W. for examination. Following this examination the Can. is placed in the W. at the l. of the S.W., facing E., to await the W.M.'s proclamation. Then follows the third and last perambulation.

8.—During the third perambulation the Can. again salutes the W.M. and J.W. as a F.C., afterwards advancing to the S.W. to communicate the P.G. and P.W. Following this examination the S.D. again places the Can. in the W. at the l. of the S.W., and places Can.'s r.h. in S.W.'s l.h. S.D. should see that Can. is facing E. and stand in line on his left. S.D. should be alert to take charge of Can. again at proper moment and stand facing E. while receiving S.W.'s directions. *No Sn. when addressed by S.W.*

9.—After directions have been given by the S.W. the S.D. conducts Can. to proper position in the N. to demonstrate method of advancing to the E. S.D. should stand in front of the Can. to address him.* The method is then demonstrated. S.D.'s position at start is with l.f. pointing towards the E. and r.f. towards the S. Start with l.f. and conclude with four distinct Sps.

10.—S.D. should remember that when the Can. is asked by the W.M. prior to the Ob. whether he

* According to Emulation practice the correct position for S.D. when addressing the Can. at this point is on the S. side of the C. There are, however, some Lodge Rooms so wide that this practice would look awkward. Here, as in other cases, Deacons will be wise to use common sense and adapt themselves to existing conditions.

is 'prepared to meet them . . .' he should answer
voluntarily.* Before the commencement of the Ob.
S.D. transfers wand to his l.h., elevates it,† takes
Sp., and shows P.Sn. of a M.M. The correct
moment to dis. Sn. is immediately the Can. repeats
the final words. *Do not forget to recover.*

11.—When the Can. has been assisted by the
W.M. the S.D. should step back with Can. and
J.D. to foot of the C.

12.—When the W.M. summons the Wardens to
assist him after the Exhortation the S.D. should wait
until the J.W. arrives immediately behind him, then
step aside and return to his seat *without squaring*.

13.—After the Charge the S.D. should *not* leave
his seat to take position beside the Can. during the
explanation of the first three Sns. S.D. should
remain seated until the W.M. informs Can. that
he 'is now at liberty to retire . . .' S.D. then conducts Can. direct and *without squaring* to left of the
S.W. and directs him how to salute the W.M. in
the three Degrees. S.D. must remember that at
this point the Can. gives only the P.Sn. of the Third
Degree. Can. then retires, the S.D. escorting him
to the door.‡ Certain matters of preparation are
now attended to by the S.D. and his colleague, and
the L.'s are restored.§

---

* See footnote on p. 133.   † See footnote on p. 132.
‡ The Can. should always be permitted to leave the Lodge
at this stage to restore himself to his p.c.'s. The slovenly
custom of completing the ceremony without allowing the Can.
to retire (on the pretext of 'saving time') is one to be deprecated
by all believers in orderly and dignified ceremonial.
§ The correct stage for restoring the L.'s is *after* the Can.
has left the Lodge to restore himself t.h.p.c. Certain words

14.—When the Can. is readmitted the S.D. meets him at the door and conducts him to the left of the S.W., directing him to salute the W.M. in the three Degrees. *Full Sns. this time.* S.D. now places Can.'s r.h. in S.W.'s l.h. for presentation to W.M. See that Can. is facing E., and stand in line with him on his left. It is the S.W.'s duty to invest the Can. with the distinguishing badge of a M.M., but the S.D. should be ready to assist if necessary.

15.—After the investiture and subsequent address the S.D. leads Can. *diagonally* (no squaring) to position from twelve to eighteen inches from the W.M.'s ped. During the T.H. the Can. should *not* be moved backward and forward as stated in some printed rituals. Such practice is contrary to Emulation-teaching.

16.—S.D. must remember that the Can. should *not* take the Sp. when the W.M. announces that 'one of the Brethren, looking round, observed . . .' S.D. should whisper to Can. to copy the Master when Sns. of H. and S. are given. A little later, when the W.M. rises to demonstrate the five Sns., the S.D. should direct Can. to take Sp. Can. copies the W.M. at each Sn., but does *not* repeat the words used by the W.M. when giving the Sns. of J. & E. and G. & D.

spoken by the W.M. during the Charge concerning 'that bright morning star' have no reference whatever to the L.'s. The undesirable practice of manipulating the electric switch at this point is obviously a modern innovation, since no such method could have been followed in the days before the introduction of electricity for lighting. The whole of the first part of the Ceremony should be performed in that state of d..k...s which we are taught in the Third Lecture alludes to the d..k...s of D...h.

17.—After explanation of the W.T.'s S.D. should conduct Can. straight to a seat and resume his own seat. The Can. should *not* be conducted to the W. to salute at the conclusion of the Ceremony.

THE CEREMONY OF PASSING

1.—During the Examination and Entrusting, prior to the Ceremony of Passing, it is the J.D. who is in charge of the Can. S.D. has no duty to perform until the Lodge has been opened in the Second Degree and the W.M. orders the admission of the Can. S.D. then takes wand in his r.h. and proceeds *without squaring* to the door, where he will be joined by the J.D. after the latter Officer has attended to the placing of the K.S.* S.D. should be watchful to see that this duty is not forgotten. S.D. conducts Can. to within a convenient distance from the K.S. and directs him to *advance* as a M.† S.D. must see that Can. takes Sp. before giving the Sn.

2.—Before the Pr. S.D. should see that the Can.'s r.h. is in correct attitude for Sn. of R. S.D. transfers wand to l.h., elevates it,‡ and places r.h. in correct attitude.

3.—After Pr. S.D. assists Can. to rise and starts on first perambulation, *squaring each corner of the Lodge.* He should bring Can. to a halt at W.M.'s ped. before directing him to salute as a M.§ Can. must again be brought to a halt at J.W.'s ped. before he is directed to advance. The S.D. does not give

* See footnote on p. 138.   † See footnote on p. 145.
‡ See footnote on p. 132.   § See footnote on p. 146.

the Sns. with the Can. at the Wardens' stations. (*See footnote on p. 135 for method of communicating the G. or T.*)

4.—After first perambulation S.D. should place Can. in the W. at l. of S.W. and await W.M.'s proclamation.

5.—Second perambulation. Can. is halted at W.M.'s and J.W.'s peds. to salute as a M., afterwards advancing to the S.W. to communicate the P.G. and P.W.

6.—After this examination the S.D. conducts the Can. to the l. of the S.W. and places Can.'s r.h. in S.W.'s l.h. S.D. should see that Can. is facing the E. and stand in line with him on his left. Be alert to take charge of Can. again at proper moment and stand facing E. while receiving S.W.'s directions. *No Sn. when addressed by S.W.*

7.—After receiving directions from the S.W. the S.D. conducts Can. to proper position in the N. to demonstrate method of advancing to the E. S.D. should stand in front of Can. to address him. The method is then demonstrated. S.D.'s position at start is with r.f. pointing towards the W. and l.f. towards the S. Commence with l.f.

8.—Before commencement of Ob. S.D. should transfer wand to l.h., elevate it,* take Sp., and show Sn. of F. The correct moment to dis. Sn. is when Can. completes the Ob. Can. should answer voluntarily when asked by W.M. if he is 'willing to take it . . .' †

9.—After the W.M. has assisted Can. to rise the

---

* See footnote on p. 132.   † See footnote on p. 133.

S.D. should place Can. at once at the right of the W.M.'s ped.   During the Entrusting the S.D. must be ready to assist if necessary, but should not interfere unduly.*   The S.D. does *not* give the Sns. as demonstrated by the W.M.   S.D. should be quick with prompt in response to W.M.'s third question, or the Can. may answer voluntarily *and incorrectly*.   When the W.M. gives the W. the S.D. repeats it to the Can., who must repeat it after him. Similar repetition when the W.M. spells the W.

10.—After the Entrusting S.D. conducts Can. to J.W.'s station for examination, *being careful to square the Lodge*.   S.D. must take Sp. and show Sn. before addressing the J.W.   Dis. Sn. before J.W. replies.† (*See para.* 3, *p.* 127, *and para.* 10, *p.* 134, *regarding the wand.*)

11.—S.D. conducts Can. to S.W.'s station for further examination.   At this point the S.D. must remember that the Can. does *not* give Sns. of a F.C. when directed to advance.‡   After this examination S.D. conducts Can. to l. of S.W. and places Can.'s r.h. in S.W.'s l.h. for presentation. S.D. should stand in line with Can. on the left.

12.—It is the S.W.'s duty to invest the Can. with the distinguishing badge of a F.C.F.M., but the S.D. should be ready to assist if necessary.   At conclusion of the S.W.'s remarks S.D. should turn Can. to face the E., standing in line on his right. After W.M.'s address regarding the badge S.D. awaits directions to conduct Can. to the S.E. corner of the Lodge.   He must be careful to remember

* See footnote on p. 134.   † See footnote on p. 135.
‡ See para. 10, p. 134.

instructions to Can. at this point. The Lodge must be *squared* when conducting Can. to S.E. corner. The correct position at the S.E. corner is just in line with the front of the W.M.'s ped.

13.—S.D. should be alert to conduct Can. to proper position at W.M.'s ped. at correct moment for explanation of the W.T.'s.

14.—When Can. is dismissed by the W.M. the S.D. should conduct him direct, *without squaring*, to the W., at the l. of the S.W., and direct him how to salute as a F.C., first as an E.A.* Can. then retires, S.D. escorting him to the door.†

15.—On the Can.'s return the S.D. meets him at the door and conducts him to l. of the S.W., directing him how to salute as a F.C., first as an E.A. S.D. now conducts Can. to foot of the T.B., which should be on the floor in the centre of the Lodge. After the Lecture on the T.B. the S.D. conducts Can. to a seat and resumes his own seat. The Can. should *not* be taken to the W. to salute after Explanation of the T.B.

THE CEREMONY OF INITIATION

1.—The S.D. is now in the position of *assistant* to his junior Brother the Junior Deacon.‡ Before the admission of the Can. the S.D. should see that

---

* See para. 5, p. 128.

† The Can. should always be permitted to leave the Lodge at this stage to restore himself to his p.c.'s. The slovenly custom of giving the Lecture on the T.B. without allowing the Can. to retire (on the pretext of 'saving time') is one to be deprecated by all believers in orderly and dignified ceremonial. ‡ See para. 1, p. 132.

the K.S. is in position. The S.D. does *not* square the Lodge when leaving his post at the right of the W.M. to attend to the K.S.* Having attended to this duty he joins the J.D. at the door to receive the Can.

2.—During the Pr. the S.D. should transfer his wand to the l.h., elevate it,† and show Sn. of R. Immediately the J.D. has assisted Can. to rise the S.D. should draw the K.S. aside * and stand in line with J.D. and Can. during the W.M.'s proclamation. The K.S. should be replaced in its position before the S.W.'s ped. directly the J.D. has started with the Can. to perambulate the Lodge. S.D. should then take the p.n...d from the S.W.'s ped. (where the I.G. should have placed it), proceed to the E., place p.n...d on W.M.'s ped., and resume his seat. It is the duty of the S.D. *and not of the I.G.* to take the p.n...d to the W.M.†

3.—When the J.D. conducts the Can. to the E. by the three irreg. sps. the S.D. should arrive there simultaneously.

4.—Before the Ob. the S.D. should assist Can. by raising his l.h. at the W.M.'s reference to the C.'s. Similarly he should lower Can.'s l.h. when the C.'s have been removed at the conclusion of the Ob. During the Ob. S.D. should transfer wand to his l.h., elevate it,† take Sp., and show P.Sn. of an E.A. The correct moment to dis. Sn. is when the Can. completes the Ob. After the W.M. has assisted Can. the S.D. resumes his seat.

* See footnote on p. 138.   † See footnote on p. 132.
‡ See footnote on p. 101.

CHAPTER XVIII

THE DIRECTOR OF CEREMONIES

As in the case of the Chaplain, Almoner, and certain other Officers of the Lodge, so with Brother Director of Ceremonies; he is not, according to the *Constitutions*, a *regular* Officer, but one of the *permissive* Officers who *may* be appointed at the will of the Worshipful Master.

It is to be assumed that in the great majority of Lodges such an appointment is always made when a competent Brother is available, ready and willing to undertake the important duties appertaining to the Office; for it may truthfully be said that a thoroughly efficient Director of Ceremonies is a boon and a blessing to the Master, and indeed to the Lodge as a whole.

There are a few (fortunately only a *very few*) Brethren who seem ever ready to disparage the Office of Director of Ceremonies, Brethren who are wont to adopt a rather lofty attitude of superior criticism towards Directors of Ceremonies. Perchance the reason for this peculiar attitude lies in the fact that at the Emulation Lodge of Improvement there is no Director of Ceremonies. The reason for the absence of a D.C. at Emulation Lodge of Improvement is simple to understand. Emulation claims to work the Ceremonies exactly as they were settled by the Lodge of Reconciliation in 1816 and to have permitted no changes or innovations during the passing of the years; and in 1816 there was no such Officer as a Director of Ceremonies in a *private Lodge*.

The first Grand Director of Ceremonies was Bro. Sir George Naylor (Garter-King-at-Arms), who was appointed in 1814, immediately after the Union, and held the Office until 1831. In 1832 he was succeeded by Bro. Sir William Woods (Garter-King-at-Arms), who officiated until 1840. From 1841 till 1859 the Office was held by Bro. Richard Jennings, who was followed from 1860 to 1904 by Bro. Sir Albert Woods, G.C.V.O., K.C.B., K.C.M.G. (Garter-King-at-Arms). Bro. Frank Richardson followed in 1904 and officiated till 1912. He was in that year succeeded by Bro. J. S. Granville Grenfell, who held the Office till 1926. Bro. Grenfell was succeeded by the present holder of the Office, Bro. Lieut.-Col. C. R. I. Nicholl.

Prior to 1915 the Grand Director of Ceremonies ranked below the Assistant Grand Superintendent of Works, and in private Lodges the D.C.'s position in the table of precedence was immediately after the Junior Deacon. At the Quarterly Communication of Grand Lodge held on 3rd March 1915 a message was received from the M.W. the Grand Master, stating that he was pleased to recommend that the holder of the Office of Grand Director of Ceremonies should rank and take precedence immediately after Past Presidents of the Board of Benevolence, and should be entitled to the prefix of 'Very Worshipful.' At the following Quarterly Communication of Grand Lodge, held on 2nd June 1915, Bro. Sir Alfred Robbins, President of the Board of General Purposes, moved the necessary resolution for the requisite amendments to the *Book of Constitutions*, which amendments made provision for the Director of Ceremonies in a private Lodge to rank immediately after the Secretary.

In private Lodges, as has been stated, there was no such Officer as D.C. in 1816, and the Office was not introduced until some years later. Therefore, the Office is non-existent at the Emulation Lodge of Improvement, and during the Installation Ceremony the duties usually falling to the lot of the D.C. are discharged by the Installing Master. At the Lodge of Improvement, of course, the Installation Ceremony is *always* conducted by an expert Past Master, one who is thoroughly conversant with Emulation practice and who knows exactly what to do; consequently the Ceremony proceeds smoothly and without a hitch.

Whether the same conditions would prevail in a private Lodge adopting similar practice is open to considerable doubt. In a few regular Lodges which

insist upon following slavishly the exact method of
the Emulation Lodge of Improvement, and work
the Installation Ceremony without a D.C., the
present writer has more than once witnessed undignified confusion and uncertainty, which would
undoubtedly have been prevented by the presence
of a competent Director of Ceremonies.

Like all other Officers of the Lodge, the Director
of Ceremonies acts under the direct authority of
the Master; yet the very nature of his Office
demands that he must be permitted to a great
extent to establish his own methods of procedure in
the discharge of his many responsibilities. The
D.C. may be regarded as the Master's adjutant and,
as such, he is of necessity vested with considerable
authority; but he should bear in mind that every
Office in the Lodge is an annual appointment, and
that, with the exception of the Treasurer and the
Tyler, the Master is free to appoint whomsoever he
pleases. It is to be presumed, however, that the
efficient Director of Ceremonies will be reappointed
year after year, and that he will gradually become
what may be considered one of the *permanent*
officials.* Fortunate indeed is the Lodge which, in
its Director of Ceremonies, has found the 'right man
in the right place.'

The qualifications desirable for the Office are
many and varied. It is essential that Brother
Director of Ceremonies should be an expert in

* See footnote on p. 119.

the Ritual of all the Ceremonies; he must be a master of such matters as Masonic Etiquette and Jurisprudence; he should be thoroughly conversant with the contents of the *Book of Constitutions*. It is advisable, too, that he should have a commanding presence, combined with a gentle, courteous demeanour, because he, more than any other Officer of the Lodge, may need to exercise the 'mailed fist' concealed within the softest of velvet gloves.

Without doubt the efficient Director of Ceremonies *must* be a Past Master, for his services (possibly his advice) will be needed during the esoteric portions of the Installation Ceremony. It has to be remembered, too, that occasions will arise when this important Officer must speak with the voice of authority; that authority must of necessity be lessened if he be not a Past Master in the Craft.

The above are but a few of the qualifications required in an efficient Director of Ceremonies; the Brother possessed of them will undoubtedly win the respect and regard, and consequently the ready obedience, of his younger Brethren.

It has to be borne in mind that none can lay down hard-and-fast rules in relation to the Director of Ceremonies and his methods in discharging the duties of his Office; much must be dependent upon Lodge customs; and much, as has already been suggested, must be left to individual discretion.

That which is favoured by one Director of Ceremonies may be frowned upon by another; but
neither would be justified in condemning the methods
of the other as *wrong*.

The newly appointed Director of Ceremonies
can only aspire to attain the degree of confident
efficiency possessed by his elder Brethren in the
school of practical experience, but it is hoped that
he may derive assistance from the following general
hints which are offered for his guidance.

GENERAL HINTS FOR THE DIRECTOR OF CEREMONIES

1.—*Before the Lodge is Opened.*

The D.C. should make a point of early arrival at all Lodge Meetings; at least a quarter of an hour before the time stated on the Summons. However expert the Tyler may be, he may make some error in setting out the Lodge. The D.C. should satisfy himself that all is in order. If there is a Ceremony to be worked the D.C. should see that the C.'s or Sq. are ready at the W.M.'s ped. He should see that the I.G.'s implements are in their place; that the columns are correctly placed, etc., etc.

In the anteroom Bro. Tyler will probably see that the Brethren sign the Attendance Book, but the D.C. should give an eye to this.

The D.C. should ascertain if all the Officers are present. If there are absentees he will probably be able to suggest efficient substitutes to the Master.

Sharp on time, if the Master and his Officers are ready, the D.C. should see that Brethren who are not in Office enter the Lodge.

2.—*Masonic Clothing, Jewels, etc.*

It is the D.C.'s duty to see that Brethren are properly clothed. White gloves should *always* be worn with evening dress, and the apron worn *under* the coat. With morning dress or dinner jackets the apron is worn *over* the coat. White gloves *should* be worn on all occasions, but some Lodges do not insist upon them. In a Craft Lodge no jewels are permissible save those appertaining to Craft or Royal Arch Masonry.

3.—*Processions into the Lodge.**

The usual procedure for the procession in London Lodges is as follows:—

D.C.

J.D.   S.D.

J.W.   S.W.

W.M.

Past Grand Stewards.

Grand Officers

(Juniors Leading).

A.D.C.

If other Brethren take part in the procession it has to be remembered that in London Lodges a Brother of London Rank takes precedence of a Provincial or

* Longer processions are sometimes formed, more particularly in Provincial Lodges. It is not uncommon in a Provincial Lodge for *all the Brethren* to take part in the processional entry. In such cases the following order is often adopted: Members of the Lodge not in Office (Juniors First), followed by:

Visiting Brethren (Juniors first).

Tyler.   I.G.

Steward.   Steward.

J.D.   S.D.

A.D.C.   D.C.

Asst. Sec.   Almoner.

Secretary.   Treasurer.

Chaplain.   I.P.M.

J.W.   S.W.

W.M.

Grand Officers (Juniors leading).

Such processions, however, are rarely seen in the Metropolitan area. Although few fixed rules can be stated, much being dependent upon Lodge or local customs, yet it may safely be said that in all *inward* processions the rule should be *juniors first*, with certain exceptions where a Brother by virtue of his particular Office takes a certain position in the procession.

THE DIRECTOR OF CEREMONIES

District Grand Officer.   In Provinces and Districts the position is reversed.

The D.C. leads the procession and at the entrance to the Lodge gives the command: 'To order, Brethren, to receive the Worshipful Master and his Wardens.' *

Slow march to the N.E.   Ranks open out and Deacons elevate their wands to form an arch beneath which the W.M. passes and is handed to his seat by the D.C.   The ranks close in and proceed, the Grand Officers dropping out to take their places. The Deacons again elevate wands at the J.W.'s station, and he passes through and is handed to his seat by the D.C.   Similarly at the S.W.'s station. At this point the J.D. drops out to take his place at the right of the S.W.   D.C. proceeds up the N. with S.D., the A.D.C. following behind.   If the Treasurer, Secretary, etc., take part in the procession it is customary for them to fall out to take their respective places as the procession moves on after the Master has been handed to his seat by the D.C.   The D.C. and A.D.C. are the last to take their stations.†

There are some experienced Directors of Ceremonies, more particularly in the Provinces, who disagree with the advice here given that in the

* In no procession should any Brother be permitted to intervene *between* the Master and his Wardens.

† No particular position in the Lodge is allotted to the D.C. or A.D.C. in the *Constitutions*, so it cannot be argued that any particular custom is either right or wrong.   For the sake of convenience it seems that the senior Officer, at any rate, should be seated somewhere in the vicinity of the Master.   It is equally convenient that the D.C. and A.D.C. should occupy adjoining seats, as the former may have to give his Assistant instructions during the evening.

processional entry the W.M. and his Wardens should precede the Grand Officers, their argument being that, as the rule for inward processions is *juniors first*, then the W.M., being senior to all other Brethren in his own Lodge, should be *behind* the Grand Officers. There is reason in the argument, and *theoretically* perhaps it is correct; but theory may sometimes be subordinated with advantage to convenience and circumstances.

In a private Lodge there are obvious objections to the Grand Officers preceding the W.M. In the event of a lengthy procession so arranged, the W.M., of course, passes through the avenue formed by the Grand Officers, and, when he has taken his place, the Grand Officers at the rear of the procession turn inward and proceed to their positions at the right of the Master's chair. The Wardens are thus left stranded somewhere in the West, perhaps for quite an appreciable period, and the D.C. must either go and fetch them or beckon them forward.

While the present writer does not for one moment presume to suggest that those who differ from his opinion are wrong, yet, from a fairly long and varied experience, he believes that the procedure he advocates avoids confusion, and results in a smoother and more dignified entry than the contrary practice.

4.—*Seating of Grand Lodge Officers*.
Grand Officers should be seated on the right of the Master *in their order of seniority*. The D.C. should memorise the table of precedence as set out in the *Book of Constitutions*. He should also be able to tell the badges of Grand Officers at a glance.

An *acting* Grand Officer of the year takes precedence over a *Past* Grand Officer of similar rank; but no acting Grand Officer takes precedence over a Past Grand Officer of *higher* rank.

5.—*General Seating.*

The seats to the E. of the Secretary's table and the J.W.'s ped. are sometimes filled up early by M.M.'s. This should not be permitted if Brethren of higher rank are present or expected to arrive later.

6.—*Entry of Grand Lodge Officers after the Lodge is Open.*

The D.C. should receive the distinguished visitor at the door, giving the order, 'To Order, Brethren,' when the Brethren rise in their places.* D.C. conducts the Grand Officer to a seat at the right of the W.M. and then gives the order, 'Be seated, Brethren.' Although in his own Lodge the Master is supreme, it is an act of courtesy for him to rise and offer his hand in greeting to the distinguished visitor.

7.—*Reception of other Visitors after the Lodge is Open.*

The D.C. or A.D.C. should see that visiting Brethren are comfortably seated according to their rank. A Brother of London or Provincial or District Rank should *not* have to search around for a seat and perhaps be crowded away in a back row.

* In many Lodges the custom prevails for the Deacons to be ordered to the door upon the arrival of a distinguished visitor. They then escort the visiting Brother to the E., the S.D. on the right and his colleague on the left. Such a custom is rare, however, in Metropolitan Lodges.

8.—*Late Arrivals generally.*

When the Lodge is getting crowded the D.C. should be alert to note where there are vacant seats. It is embarrassing for a visiting Brother arriving late —and possibly during an important Ceremony— not to be able to find a seat. Whatever the visitor's Masonic rank the D.C. should be alert to assist him in finding a seat.

9.—*Visitors from Foreign Constitutions.*

There is always the possibility of a Brother arriving as a Visitor from a Lodge under the jurisdiction of a foreign Grand Lodge, and doubt may arise as to whether he may be admitted. *The greatest care is essential!* No Brother may be admitted unless he be a member of a Lodge working under a Grand Lodge recognised by the United Grand Lodge of England.

10.—*Salutes to Grand Officers.*

Such salutes are best given in the highest Degree in which the Lodge is to be opened. If in the Third Degree, then with the G. or R. Sn. It is a common error to salute with the G. or R. Sn. in the First or Second Degree. This is *absolutely wrong.*

The correct salutes to Grand Officers within the Lodge are as follows:

M.W.G.M. or M.W.ProG.M. . .	11
R.W.D.G.M.	9
R.W. Brethren	7
V.W. Brethren	5
Other Grand Officers	3

* Provincial Grand Officers:

R.W.Prov.G.M. 7
W. Dep. Prov. G.M. (in their own Province) 5
W. Asst. Prov. G.M. (in their own Province) 5
Other Prov. Grand Officers (in their own
      Province) 3

No Brother while acting in a higher Office may receive a salute other than that to which he is personally entitled.

Having ascertained the wishes of the W.M., and decided upon the convenient time for the salute, the D.C. gives the order: 'To order, Brethren,' or 'Upstanding, Brethren,' when the Brethren rise. D.C. proceeds: 'By command of the W.M. I call upon you to salute the Grand Lodge Officers with three, taking the time from me! To order, Brethren!' The salute is then given. After the salute the D.C. says: 'Be seated, Brethren.' The senior Grand Officer then acknowledges the greeting. (NOTE.—This is, of course, assuming that all the Grand Officers present are below the rank of Grand Inspector.)

11.—*Ceremonial Address.*

The present and past Grand Masters and the present and past Pro Grand Masters are entitled to the appellation of 'Most Worshipful' (M.W.). The present and past Deputy Grand Masters, the present and past Provincial and District Grand Masters, and the present and past Grand Wardens of Grand Lodge are entitled to the prefix 'Right Worshipful' (R.W.).

* The table of salutes to Provincial Grand Officers applies also to District Grand Officers.

The present and past Grand Chaplains, present and past Grand Treasurers, present and past Grand Registrars, present and past Deputy Grand Registrars, present and past Presidents of the Board of General Purposes, present and past Grand Secretaries, present and past Presidents of the Board of Benevolence, present and past Grand Directors of Ceremonies, and the present and past Grand Inspectors are entitled to the prefix 'Very Worshipful' (V.W.). The address of 'Worshipful' (W.) is used by the rest of the Grand Officers, present and past, and by the present and past Masters of Lodges. All other Brethren are designated as 'Brother' only.

12.—*Masonic Applause.*

The only form of Masonic applause permissible is a single clap, but even this is better omitted unless the custom of the Lodge and the wishes of the W.M. ordain otherwise. In any case it should only be given on the command of the D.C., who should stand and let his hands be seen by all, so that the clap may be simultaneous.

13.—*Salutes and Greetings.*

At the Emulation Lodge of Improvement the salutes (or greetings) given during the Installation Ceremony or to Grand Officers are given very audibly. The theory advanced is that there is a difference between '*salutes*' and '*greetings*'—that all *salutes* should be *silent*, while all *greetings* should be *audible* and hearty. There may be much in the theory, but the fact remains that audible and noisy salutes are frowned upon by the Officials of Grand

Lodge, as may be seen at any Consecration Meeting. Directors of Ceremonies must use their own discretion as to whether they accept the theory advanced by the Committee of Emulation Lodge of Improvement or whether they prefer to bow to the example of the Grand Director of Ceremonies and his Deputies.*

14.—*When Opening the Lodge in the Second or Third Degree.*

Possibly the W.M. may omit to request E.A.'s or F.C.'s to retire. The D.C. should be on the alert to see that this is always done.

15.—*Prompting in Lodge.*

All prompting in Lodge should be avoided unless it be essential; but the occasion may arise when both the W.M. and the I.P.M. are at a loss. It is the D.C. who should be able to supply the necessary cue quietly and as unobtrusively as possible.

---

* Since publication of the first edition of this Manual the statement has been widely circulated that the late V.W. Bro. J. S. Granville Grenfell (G.D.C. for fourteen years) did *not* favour the silent method of giving the salutes. The author has, therefore, been at some trouble to place the matter beyond all dispute, and has been in communication, not only with the present Grand Director of Ceremonies, but also with the Brethren who officiated as Deputy Grand Directors of Ceremonies during Bro. Grenfell's long period of office. Of the past D.G.D.'s of C.'s only one (a Brother who officiated sixteen years ago and who is a past Preceptor of a recognised Emulation-working L.I.) states that he favours the audible salute, and it has to be noted that even this Brother does *not* suggest that he was ever directed to follow such method by the G.D.C. The other Brethren concerned, including the present G.D.C., seem quite unanimous in their opinion that the late Bro. Grenfell favoured the silent salute and directed his Deputies to give it in that manner.

16.—*The D.C.'s Wand.*

In Lodge the D.C. should not move about without his wand. Many expert D.C.'s are able to give all Sns. and salutes without relieving themselves of their wands, but if in certain cases the D.C. feels that he *must* put his wand aside temporarily when salutes are to be given, then he should place it in its stand. To surrender the wand to another's keeping, even for a few minutes, looks, to say the least of it, amateurish and undignified.

17.—*Proving unknown Visitors.*

In the event of an unknown visitor requesting admission it will probably fall to the lot of the D.C. to 'prove' him. He should always be prepared to discharge this duty in a thorough manner. It can never be *too thorough*.

18.—*The Installation Ceremony.*

The D.C. should conduct the P.M.'s who are to occupy the positions of S.W., J.W., and I.G.

After the opening of the Lodge in the Second Degree the D.C. presents the Master - Elect. Remember NOT *Worshipful* Master-Elect.*

It is a good plan for the D.C. to arrange with the Tyler that when the M.M.'s are readmitted to the Lodge the Visiting Brethren are requested by the Tyler to enter first, the Members waiting behind for a few moments. The Visitors having entered the Lodge and taken their seats,† the Members can

---

* There being no D.C. at the Emulation Lodge of Improvement, this duty is discharged by the I.M. (See p. 155.)

† At Emulation Lodge of Improvement there is *no salute* by the Brethren when re-entering the Lodge at this point, but it must be remembered that Emulation is, in fact, a Lodge

then enter and be marshalled in the North by the D.C. or A.D.C. for the perambulation, without trouble or confusion.

The D.C. should remember to attend to the changing of the T.B.'s when there is no longer a J.D. available to do it.

When the M.M.'s are ordered to retire the D.C. should see that any Officers who are leaving the Lodge leave their collars on their seats.*

According to the Emulation system the Brethren do *not* salute when ordered to retire from the Lodge. A reason for the absence of the salute which the author has heard advanced by one of Emulation's senior and most experienced Preceptors is that, directly the W.M. requests the Brethren to retire, it is the I.G.'s duty to open the door. Therefore, the door being open, the Lodge is not properly tyled, and no Masonic Sn. should be shown. Quite sound reasoning.

of Instruction, and that there is little difference, if any, between Members and Visitors; at Emulation, Visitors do, as a matter of fact, take part in the perambulation. Although, for the sake of convenience, some of the Brethren at Emulation are permitted to be seated on re-entering the Lodge, it is *assumed* that *all* are about to pass round the Lodge to salute the W.M. Therefore, the Brethren do *not* salute on re-entry. In a Regular Lodge the same conditions do not prevail; custom dictates in most Lodges that Visiting Brethren proceed to their seats and are excused from taking part in the perambulation, and the question arises: Should they salute? The author ventures to answer the query with an unhesitating affirmative, although he in no way questions the propriety of the procedure at Emulation. The conditions at the Lodge of Improvement and in a regular Lodge are, as stated, quite different.

* The W.M. has *no power* to declare 'All Offices Vacant.' See para. 4, p. 245, and para. 15, p. 224.

During the Closings in Third and Second Degrees the D.C. should keep an eye on the emblems on the V.S.L. It is quite possible that the newly invested I.P.M. may forget to attend to them.

Where there is a capable A.D.C. who is a P.M. it is sometimes the custom for him to head the column for each perambulation when the M.M.'s, F.C.'s, and E.A.'s pass round the Lodge to salute the W.M. When this custom is adopted it is the D.C. who should give the greetings from the S.E. corner of the Lodge. The Brethren should *not* be directed to salute the W.M. 'in passing.' *

In Emulation-working there is *no squaring* of the Lodge when the D.C. conducts the newly invested Officers to their stations.† In most other systems the Lodge is so squared.‡

The D.C. should on no account omit to conduct the Tyler to and from the W.M.'s ped. with the same courtesy extended to other Officers of the Lodge.§

19.—*Procession out of the Lodge.*

In the majority of London Lodges it is customary in the outgoing procession for the W.M. to *precede* his Wardens. The order for a short procession is as follows :—

---

* See footnote on p. 146.

† After escorting the newly invested Wardens and I.G. to their respective stations the D.C. should remember to conduct the P.M.'s who have been acting as temporary Officers to seats in accordance with their rank.

‡ See Chapter VI, ' Squaring the Lodge.'

§ This is not so done by the I.M. at the Emulation Lodge of Improvement, which seems an unfortunate omission of fraternal attention to an Officer who is none the less worthy of courtesy because he happens to be a Serving Brother.

A.D.C.

J.D.   S.D.

W.M.

J.W.   S.W.

Grand Officers

(Seniors First).

Past Grand Stewards.

Officers of London Rank.

Prov. or Dist. Grand Officers.*

P.M.'s.

D.C.

Many Provincial Lodges favour longer processions. A safe rule to follow for *outgoing* processions is *Seniors First.*†

Either immediately before the procession leaves the Lodge, or in the anteroom (according to custom), it is usual for the D.C. to announce the W.M.'s commands as to whether the Brethren are to 'Dine in Collars,' etc.‡

20.—*At Refreshment.*

The D.C. should be early in the dining-room and keep a watchful eye on the arrangements to see that all Brethren are comfortably accommodated and seated according to their rank. At Refreshment, as at Labour, due observance should be paid to Masonic etiquette. Grand Lodge Officers and other

* In Provinces or Districts Provincial or District Grand Officers take precedence over Officers of London Rank.

† D.C. brings up rear of the procession, it being his duty to see that all others take their correct positions.

‡ If the banquet be held in a building other than that in which the Lodge Meeting is held Masonic Clothing may **not** be worn unless by Dispensation.

distinguished guests should (unless amicable arrangements be made to the contrary) be seated strictly according to their seniority. Similar considerations should also be observed when calling upon them for responses to toasts.

Lack of space forbids that the foregoing list should be extended, and this chapter must close with a final reminder to Brother Director of Ceremonies that his Office is essentially one of *command*. He should remember to combine firmness and dignity with tact and gentleness. All commands should be given distinctly, but without undue shouting; to be too loud is to risk conveying a hint of arrogance.

A quiet dignity in the execution of his duties earns the Director of Ceremonies respect and obedience. He should ever be careful to remember that the Worshipful Master reigns supreme; there should never be the slightest suggestion that the Director of Ceremonies is endeavouring to *rule* the Lodge.

All men do well to hold a high ideal ever before them, and the newly invested Director of Ceremonies cannot do better than attend the Quarterly Communications of Grand Lodge, there to study the methods of the Grand Director of Ceremonies, V.W. Bro. C. R. I. Nicholl. It was the present writer's good fortune to receive many invaluable hints from the late V.W. Bro. J. S. Granville Grenfell, who held the Office of Grand Director of Ceremonies from 1912 until 1926, a revered Brother who combined courtly bearing with gentle firmness, and one who surely raised his responsible Office to the highest possible heights of dignified efficiency. Needless to say, his distinguished successor worthily upholds that standard. Directors of Ceremonies cannot do better than strive to attain a modicum of his knowledge and ability.

CHAPTER XIX

THE SECRETARY

IT would be difficult to over-estimate the importance attaching to the Office of Brother Secretary, whose station is in the North, and whose distinctive Jewel is 'two pens in saltire.' The ceremonial address delivered to him by the Master upon his investiture comprises a meagre two dozen words. In some Lodges it is extended slightly, Brother Secretary being reminded that his Office is 'one of considerable importance.' The Emulation Ritual, however, omits this reminder, possibly on the grounds that the Brother who has to shoulder so many responsibilities is fully aware of the importance attaching thereto.

Only once during the year is the Secretary called upon by virtue of his Office to take any part in the ceremonial proceedings of the Lodge—at the Installation Meeting when he calls the attention of the Master-Elect to the Ancient Charges and Regulations. Yet the Secretary is, without doubt, the hardest worked of all the Officers.

If there be younger Brethren inclined at times to speak rather thoughtlessly of Brother Secretary 'bossing' the Lodge let them pause for quiet reflection. Let them ponder upon the smoothness and dispatch with which the Lodge meetings proceed; the certainty and readiness with which helpful advice is instantly forthcoming when the Master finds himself in any doubt or difficulty; the regularity with which all members receive their Lodge Summons and other communications; the arrangements made for their comfort during Refreshment; the happy success of the Ladies' Festival or annual Summer Outing. Let them ponder over these and many other matters and ask themselves to whom their thanks are due.

That the Secretary should be an experienced Past Master goes without saying; he will, in the course of his duties, have to deal with many matters requiring knowledge which a young and inexperienced Brother cannot be expected to possess.

In a Lodge which is fortunate enough to have in its Scribe a popular and experienced Past Master who has the interests of the Lodge at heart, the Brethren are not likely to desire to see any change made in the occupancy of the Office. Hence Brother Secretary is, more often than not, reappointed from year to year, and generally regarded as the 'permanent official' of the Lodge.* This fact, however, gives him no *right* to reappointment. Theoretically, at any rate, he holds his Office for but one year; he is, in common with all the Officers,

* See footnote on p. 119.

12

subordinate to the Master who appointed him; and the next Master is at perfect liberty to displace him without giving reasons for so doing. Such a contingency, however, is unlikely if the Secretary be the right man in the right place, as, happily, he so often is.

Obviously one of Brother Secretary's most important duties is the recording in the Minute Book of such of the proceedings at the Lodge Meetings as are proper to be written. Experience alone can teach him how best to chronicle those proceedings in a manner which combines desirable brevity with satisfactory completeness of record.

An infringement of the *Constitutions* for which Secretaries are sometimes responsible, even in these enlightened days, is the omission from the Minute Book of the names of all the Brethren present. One often hears Brother Secretary read the names of the Master, Officers, and Visitors, and add: ". . . and the Brethren whose names are duly recorded in the Attendance Book." Such a practice is a direct violation of the *Constitutions*. By permission of the Master a long list of names may be 'taken as read,' but Rule 172, *Book of Constitutions*, definitely states that the Secretary *must* enter in the Minutes: "The names of all members present at each meeting of the Lodge, together with those of all visiting Brethren, with their Lodges and Masonic rank."

At each Regular Lodge Meeting the Minutes of the last Regular Meeting, together with those of any intervening Emergency Meetings, should be read by the Secretary and, if duly confirmed, signed by the Master. Minutes cannot be confirmed at an Emergency Meeting; such a meeting is called for a distinct, emergent purpose, which must be clearly stated in the Summons, and no other business may be entered upon. (See Rules 166 and 172, *B. of C.**)

The question of the confirmation (or non-confirmation) of the Minutes is one which, at various times and in various places, has given rise to much discussion and argument. Actually, the only question at issue is as to the *accuracy of record.*† If the Minutes contain an *accurate record* of the proceedings they should be confirmed, although, be it noted, the confirming of the Minutes does not *ipso facto* legalise all the proceedings referred to therein. Acceptance of the Minutes, then, merely signifies that Brother Secretary has accurately recorded the happenings at the meeting to which they refer.

There are some matters, of course, which, by their very nature, or perhaps in compliance with the Lodge By-Laws, require confirmation at a subsequent meeting. Such matters should be made the subject of a separate motion set out on the Agenda. If, during the interval between one meeting and another, Brethren have changed their minds, their procedure is to vote against the motion

* See para. 6, p. 247, and p. 237 under " The Risings."
† See Chapter XXVI, p. 219.

to confirm the previous resolution. On the other hand, any matter which is in itself complete, and does not require a confirmatory vote, cannot be vetoed by any mere non-confirmation of the Minutes. In such a case any alteration must be effected by a fresh substantive motion, of which notice must be given, to rescind the previous resolution.

There is an instance on record of the Grand Lodge upholding the ruling of a District Grand Master that a proposition for non-confirmation of Minutes cannot be made merely for the purpose of allowing Brethren to revise their opinions. As stated, the only question at issue is the *accuracy of record* by the Secretary.

In addition to reading the Minutes of preceding meetings, and noting all important happenings at the present meeting, the Secretary's duties in Lodge will include the reading of Grand Lodge and other communications, and perhaps reporting to the Lodge upon various matters which may have been entrusted to his experienced care at the previous meeting.

The major portion of the Secretary's duties, however, are discharged away from the Lodge and necessitate the sacrifice of much of his personal leisure. The following is a typical quotation from Lodge By-Laws relating to the duties of the Secretary :—

"The Secretary shall, under the direction of the Master, give every Member of the Lodge at least seven days' notice of all Regular Meetings, and, in case of emergency, such other notice as is required by the *Book of Constitutions*, and shall insert in such notices the nature of all business to be transacted.

" He shall attend all the Meetings of the Lodge, and shall keep Minutes of all proceedings and business such as are proper to be written, which Minutes shall be read at the next Regular Meeting, when the Brethren shall either confirm or amend them.

" He shall file a copy of all Summonses convening the Meetings; make out all Returns for Grand Lodge; inform every Member the amount of all subscriptions and fees due; collect all fees and subscriptions and pay same over to the Treasurer; send a copy of the Balance Sheet annually to every Subscribing Member, together with a list of the Members and their addresses and dates of Initiation or Joining; and keep an inventory of the Lodge property."

This quotation is sufficient to give some indication as to the many and varied responsibilities devolving upon our Brother Secretary. The list might be considerably extended, but it will suffice to show that the Scribe's Office is no sinecure.

In view of the many claims made upon him, and the amount of time he must expend on his duties away from the Lodge, many Lodges provide in their By-Laws that Brother Secretary shall be exempt from the payment of the annual subscription. Such exemption is sanctioned in the *Book of Constitutions*, but Rule 235 makes it clear that in such cases Secretaries "shall be considered in all respects as regular subscribing members of their Lodges, their services being equivalent to subscription, provided their dues to the Grand Lodge have been paid." In this connection it may be noted that no such exemption may be granted to any other Officer. Nor may Brother Secretary be designated as 'Honorary Secretary'; the term 'Secretary' is alone recognised by the Constitutions.

An important point which the Secretary will do well to remember is that, under the laws attaching to Employers' Liability, a Lodge is liable in the case of accident and injury to the Tyler while engaged in his duties or travelling to and from the Lodge. This has been definitely established, and the Secretary is neglectful of the Lodge's interests if he omits to see that a few shillings are expended annually on a protective insurance policy. Protection against fire and burglary is usually provided for in Lodge By-Laws.

To be successful Brother Secretary must bring to bear upon the execution of his duties a considerable amount of tact, patience, perseverance, and a keen understanding of human nature. It may be irksome—no doubt it is—for an experienced Secretary to have to endure what he may regard as unnecessary 'interference' from a young and inexperienced Master. Yet it has to be remembered that the Master *is* the Master and, as such, his word is law. Tact may overcome many difficulties. However experienced he may be, the Secretary should avoid any suggestion of endeavouring to *rule* the Master and the Lodge. It is his duty to consult the Master upon all matters; certainly no Lodge Summons should ever be sent out until a draft has been submitted to the Master for approval. It is by such proper recognition of the Master's authority that difficulties are avoided and harmony maintained.

We have somewhere seen the following lines anent Brother Secretary:—

"If he writes a letter, it is too long; if he sends a post-card, it is too short; if he attends a Committee, he is butting in; if he stays away, he is a shirker; if the attendance is small at Lodge, he should have whipped the members up; if he *does* do so, he is a nuisance; if he presses a member for his dues, he is insulting; if he does not, he is lazy; if a function is a great success, praise is due to the Committee; if it is a failure, the Secretary is to blame; if he asks for suggestions, he is incompetent; if he does not, he is pig-headed."

There is a lot of truth in it, yet, in the majority of cases, Brother Secretary will carry on as heretofore, cheerfully contributing to the comfort of his Brethren and proving himself a tower of strength to the Worshipful Master.

It will be noticed that no guiding hints are offered to aid Brother Secretary in the discharge of his duties; in all probability he knows them better than we do.

CHAPTER XX

THE TREASURER

BROTHER TREASURER shares with his Brother the Tyler the distinction of being an *elected* Officer of the Lodge. Neither of these Brethren depend for their Office upon the favour of the Master; they are elected thereto by the votes of their Brethren in Open Lodge assembled. The Treasurer ranks high in the table of precedence, taking position immediately after the Chaplain and before the Secretary. His Jewel of Office is the Key, emblematical in its material sense of the guardianship of the Lodge chest.

The Treasurer having no part in the ceremonial proceedings, there is little that need be said about his Office in this Manual. That is not to say that the Office is one of minor importance. The occupant of the Office is generally a Past Master of many years' standing, and the mere fact that he is *elected*, and not *appointed* by the Master, is sufficient evidence that he holds the confidence and regard of his Brethren. Election to this Office is, quite rightly, regarded as no slight honour.

Perhaps the most useful hint which can be offered

to Brother Treasurer is that he should at all times adopt a moderate and fraternal attitude in his dealings with the Brother with whom he will be brought into most intimate contact. We refer, of course, to Brother Secretary. It is an unfortunate truth that these two vitally important officials do not *always* work in complete harmony. The duties of each should be clearly defined in the Lodge By-Laws, and there should be no occasion for any hint of friction between them. In the majority of cases it is the Secretary who is responsible for the collection of all monies due to the Lodge, which sums he subsequently passes over to his colleague.

In the case of payments varying customs prevail. In some cases cheques are signed by the Treasurer alone; in others the Secretary countersigns the cheques. The policy of two signatures appears to be the wiser practice. Whichever custom may obtain, the Treasurer should never adopt an attitude of 'superiority' in his dealings with his coadjutor.

Without in any way belittling the Office of Brother Treasurer, still he may be reminded that his responsibilities and worries are, in the majority of cases, dwarfed into insignificance when compared with those of Brother Secretary. Each of these responsible Officers is, in all probability, a senior Past Master of long experience. As such they should long since have come to appreciate the significance of the first of the Three Grand Principles upon which our Order is founded. Brothers Treasurer and Secretary should, in the interests of the Lodge, cultivate and maintain at all times the most friendly and fraternal of relations.

CHAPTER XXI

THE CHAPLAIN

RULE 18, *Book of Constitutions*, states that the Grand Master *shall* appoint certain Officers, and the list given includes 'Two Grand Chaplains.' Rule 87 states that a Provincial or District Grand Master '*is empowered*' to appoint certain Provincial or District Grand Officers, and again the list includes 'Two Chaplains.' Rule 129 states that the Master of a private Lodge '*may*' appoint a Chaplain.

It will therefore be seen that our Reverend Brother the Chaplain is not a *regular* Officer. His is one of the seven *permissive* Offices which **may** be filled by the Master of a private Lodge. When so filled the Chaplain's position in the table of precedence is quite rightly a high one, coming immediately after the Junior Warden and before the Treasurer.

The description of the Chaplain's Jewel of Office, as set out in the *Constitutions*, is 'a book within a triangle surmounting a glory.' This Jewel serves to emphasise the importance of the Office of its wearer, for the 'book' referred to is the V.S.L.,

187

the first of the Three Great Masonic Lights, a *Landmark* of the Order without which no Lodge may be opened.

Needless to say, the Office with which we are for the moment concerned is one best occupied by a Minister of Religion. The question as to whether it is advisable, in the absence of a Reverend Brother, to appoint a layman to the Office, is one which has provoked much discussion. Many hold the opinion that, generally speaking, it were better *not* to follow such a course; but the question is one which must be left to the discretion of individual Masters.

By common consent the position of our Brother Chaplain in Lodge is near the Master, generally the seat on the left of the Immediate Past Master. In many Lodges the same position at the dinner-table is regarded as the Chaplain's right, although, if our Reverend Brother be not a Past Master, he will, perhaps, be acting wisely not to obtrude himself in a position prior to lay Brethren who are his seniors in the Craft.

The Chaplain's duties in Lodge are obvious —to offer Prayer to the G.A.O.T.U.,—and those duties need not be dilated upon at length. Suffice it to say that there should be perfect understanding between the Worshipful Master and the Chaplain,* and that our Reverend Brother *must* be letter-perfect, possessing sufficient knowledge of the Ritual to enable him to know *without prompting* the

* See para. 5, p. 234.

precise moment at which his voice should be heard. Nothing detracts more from the dignity and impressiveness of the proceedings than those unfortunate pauses which occur when the inexperienced Chaplain 'misses his cue,' stumbling and faltering, at a loss to find the solemn words which should have been ready to his tongue.

Apart from praise to the G.A.O.T.U. there are certain portions of the Ceremonies which may with advantage be confided to the Chaplain if he possess the requisite Masonic knowledge. The Charge to the Candidate after Initiation is but one instance. Assuming Brother Chaplain to be a Minister of Religion, he is by virtue of his training a scholar, and, it is to be hoped, an accomplished elocutionist. The Entered Apprentice's Charge may be entrusted to such a Brother with the certainty of Profit and Pleasure as the result, both to the newly initiated Brother and to all others present.

Outside the Lodge the Chaplain who has the interests of the Craft at heart will no doubt find many directions for the outlet of his Masonic energies. The duty of visiting Brethren absent through sickness is one which he may well take upon himself.

In the best regulated of Lodges little differences of opinion will unfortunately occur at times among the Brethren; and, if they be left unchecked, they may assume dimensions likely to cause something in the nature of a 'split' in the Lodge. Brother

Chaplain, by nature a man of peace, may do much to heal such differences by a few kindly, tactful words. Such mediation, coming from a Minister of Religion, will often be accepted where it might possibly be resented from others.

There can be no doubt that the Chaplain who is possessed of extensive Masonic experience, in addition to a wide knowledge of human nature, is a valuable acquisition to any Lodge. The Master whose list of Officers includes such a Brother is to be congratulated upon his good fortune.

CHAPTER XXII

THE WARDENS

IT would be difficult to lay too great an emphasis upon the fact that any successful and well-conducted Lodge must of necessity have in its Wardens two Brethren who are not merely experienced in the mysteries of the Craft, but Brethren who, by their personal conduct, are fitted in every way to be regarded as examples to their younger Brethren.

There is much to be learnt from the symbolism of the Jewels worn by these two highly placed Officers of the Lodge. The distinguishing Jewel of our Brother the Senior Warden is the Level, an emblem of the impartial and equitable conduct which should characterise all his dealings with his Brethren. His junior Brother is known by the familiar Plumb Rule, the symbol of integrity and uprightness. Happy the Lodge whose Wardens endeavour to live up to the moral teachings of their respective insignia; and happy the master who has the support of such lieutenants in the West and South.

The Wardens occupy positions of responsibility nearly equal to that of the Master himself, and, while it is an oft-repeated assertion that the power of the

Master is supreme, yet there is much evidence to be found to support the equally familiar statement that the Lodge is ruled by the Master *and* his Wardens. Certain it is that the work of any Lodge would be at a standstill without the efficient co-operation of the Wardens.

During the Installation Ceremony, if it be correctly rendered, the D.C. asks: 'W.M., whom do you appoint *your* Senior Warden?' In the case of the Senior Deacon the inquiry is: 'Whom do you appoint Senior Deacon?' The word '*your*' is omitted. To the Warden upon investiture the Master says: 'Bro. A. B., I appoint you *my* Senior Warden.' To the Deacon he says: 'I appoint you Senior Deacon *of the Lodge.*' The difference is worthy of notice.

Rule 129, *Book of Constitutions*, states that: "The regular Officers of a Lodge consist of the Master and *his* two Wardens, a Treasurer, a Secretary . . ." The possessive case is emphasised to indicate the close personal connection existing between Master and Wardens. It may fairly be assumed that, to a great extent, the control of the Lodge is presumed to be vested in the Master *and* his Wardens. Brother Dr A. G. Mackey, whose prolific pen produced Masonic writings almost rivalling in number those of the famous Bro. Dr Oliver, included in his list of additional Antient Landmarks of the Order—'*Government of a Lodge by the Master and his Wardens.*' Therefore, these three highly placed Officers should always present a united front; in a well-ordered Lodge there should never be the slightest suspicion of lack of unanimity between Master and Wardens.

No Brother has any *claim* to progress from one Office to another,* but it may fairly be assumed that when the Master appoints his Senior Warden he is designating his successor. For that reason, if for no other, the greatest care is essential in filling that important Office. In the case of the selection of the Junior Warden the responsibility is almost as great, for it has to be remembered that the appointment carries with it the necessary qualification for the future occupancy of the Chair of K.S.

Although no *claim* to progress is recognised, it cannot be disputed that every Brother has a right to aspire to the occupancy of the exalted position in the East. The Warden, whether he be Senior or Junior, is very near to the fulfilment of his ambition, and he owes it to his Lodge and to the Craft that he should be conscientious in the discharge of his important duties.

Wardens have many duties beyond the mere repetition of their somewhat limited portions of the Ritual; that may, perhaps, be regarded as the least of their responsibilities. It is the duty of the Warden to know a good deal regarding the contents of the *Book of Constitutions*. Even at personal inconvenience he should make opportunity to attend the

* See footnote on p. 111.

Quarterly Communications of the Grand Lodge because it is his duty, as a prospective ruler in the Craft, to know what is happening there. He should also be familiar with the intricacies of Masonic Jurisprudence. Wardens should cultivate tact and dignity. They should remember, too, that it is no small part of their duty to attain to some degree of competence as speakers.

This last is of greater importance than may be apparent at a glance. It has to be remembered that the Warden is likely soon to be the Master, and that much of the dignity of the Lodge proceedings must depend upon the Master's powers of oratory. Even the most nervous and halting of speakers may make marked improvement if he will but take the trouble —when he knows he is likely to be called upon to address his Brethren—to spend a little time beforehand in thinking of *what* he is going to say and *how* he is going to say it. To the Brother who has been wise enough to prepare his remarks in his early Masonic days there may come the time when, finding himself called on for an impromptu speech, he will have cause to be surprised at his own success, although he may not then realise that he owes that success entirely to the trouble and care he has taken in the past.

The responsibilities of the Wardens do not end with the closing of the Lodge; at Refreshment,* as

---

* The period of Refreshment should *never* be referred to as the ' Fourth Degree.'

at Labour, they are the Master's chief Officers, and, as such, they should do their share towards preserving the dignity and harmony of the proceedings. It is an unfortunate truth which has to be faced that the proceedings at the social board are not always characterised by proper decorum. In many Lodges the custom of 'challenging' is frequently carried to excess. Brethren are on their feet every few minutes shouting across the room, and an atmosphere of undignified uproar prevails. The Master, of course, is chiefly responsible for maintaining order, but the Wardens presiding in the West and South may do much to assist him in this connection. No Warden would wish to assume the rôle of a 'kill-joy,' but it is his *duty* to check anything in the nature of undue hilarity and noisy behaviour.

At Refreshment, as at Labour, the Wardens should be prompt in answering the Master's ⎯▆. And here Brother Warden may be reminded that there is no need, either in Lodge or at the banquet, to exert undue force in the use of the ⎯▆. Such force is frequently exerted, more particularly at the dinner-table; peace is disturbed by a series of resounding crashes which set the glasses jingling and often result in the spilling of wine. Such heavy gavelling is quite unnecessary and is a trial to the nerves.

The question as to whether the Wardens should *always* be upstanding when the Master rises to propose a toast is one upon which there is a divergence of opinion. It is a widely followed custom for the Master to make the preliminary inquiry: 'Brother Senior and Junior Wardens, how do you report the glasses under your respective columns?' Upon receiving the assurance: 'All charged in the West (or South), Worshipful Master,' he gives the order: 'Please attend the charge,' or 'Principal Officers upstanding.' Thus the Wardens are supporting the Master, and, in effect, the toast is submitted by the three Principal Officers of the Lodge.

Frequently, however, the Master omits the inquiry or command referred to, in which case one sometimes sees the Wardens rise voluntarily, while in other cases they remain seated. In the latter case we frequently see Brother Director of Ceremonies or some other Brother excitedly signalling to the Wardens to rise. In the opinion of the present writer this is quite incorrect. If the Master himself does not call upon his Principal Officers to rise certainly no other Brother has the right to *usurp the Master's powers* by so doing. It seems equally undesirable for the Wardens to rise voluntarily; it can only be regarded as an intimation that the Master is negligent and has omitted a part of his duty. The wisest course is for the Wardens to come to a definite understanding with the Master beforehand.

In many large Lodges a Brother has to wait several years before attaining the coveted dignity of a Warden's chair, and it is to be expected that such Brethren will have gained much experience in the science of Freemasonry before their appointment. In these days of Masonic expansion, however, there are new Lodges coming into existence practically every week and comparatively young Masons find themselves elevated to the responsible stations in the West and South. For the benefit of such of our younger Brethren some guiding hints are offered in the following chapters.

CHAPTER XXIII

THE JUNIOR WARDEN

REPRESENTATIVE of Hiram Abiff, Brother Junior Warden is the third Officer of the Lodge, occupying a position scarcely less responsible than that of his senior colleague. His station is in the South. His distinctive Jewel, the Plumb Rule, is the emblem of Uprightness and Integrity. His column, that of the Corinthian Order, is symbolic of Beauty; it should be kept horizontal while the Lodge is at Labour, and always raised when the Lodge is Called Off or Closed.

Brother Junior Warden should remember that no Lodge meeting can be *adjourned*. Under the English Constitution no Lodge—not even the Grand Lodge itself—has power to adjourn a meeting. The days of Regular Meetings of all Private Lodges must be *fixed and approved* by the Grand Lodge authorities, confirmation from that authority being essential before any change may be made. Masters of Private Lodges may call Lodges of Emergency,* but at every meeting, be it Regular or Emergent, the Lodge must be Opened *and Closed*. The Lodge being

* See para. 6, p. 247.

closed, the meeting cannot possibly be *adjourned*. It is, therefore, quite incorrect for the Junior Warden to state that the meeting is adjourned.

All reports are first announced by the Inner Guard to the Junior Warden, the latter Officer being nominally responsible for the admission of all Brethren, be they Members or Visitors. Perhaps it seldom happens in a London Lodge that the Junior Warden is called upon to leave his chair and proceed to the anteroom for the purpose of 'proving' a Visiting Brother; but he is liable at any time to be directed to undertake that duty. Every Junior Warden should know how to 'prove' a stranger.

It is to be assumed that even the comparatively young Mason who has made sufficient progress to enable him to reach the dignified and important position of Junior Warden will have acquired the necessary knowledge to make him thoroughly familiar with the duties of that Office so far as they relate to the Opening and Closing of the Lodge in the Three Degrees. Those duties, therefore, will not be dealt with here, but hints are appended for the guidance of Brother Junior Warden during the Ceremonies of Initiation, Passing, and Raising.

THE CEREMONY OF INITIATION

1.—Upon the announcement from the I.G. that t.i.a.r., the J.W. should give three slow and deliberate ⏤❚ *while seated*. He then rises, takes Sp., shows

Sn. of E.A., and reports to the W.M.* Upon receiving the W.M.'s reply the J.W. should dis. Sn. smartly, keeping the h. *open*, resume seat, and give necessary directions to I.G.

2.—When the Can. is taken to the J.W. by the J.D. the J.W. should remain seated until J.D. has replied: 'By t.h.o.G.b.f.a.o.g.r.' J.W. then rises, takes Can.'s r.h., says, 'Enter, f.a.o.g.r.,' and resumes seat.

3.—At the point where the Can. is restored to L...t the Wardens should *not* use ▬{. Their action here should be similar to that of the rest of the Brethren.

4.—Later when the Can. is again taken to the J.W., after he has been entrusted by the W.M. with the Ss. of the Degree, the J.W. should remain seated until the Can. has answered that he has something to communicate. J.W. then rises, takes Sp., and proceeds with examination. J.W. should *not* give the G. or T. until it has first been given by the Can. At conclusion of examination J.W. says, 'Pass . . . .' and resumes his seat.

THE CEREMONY OF PASSING

1.—Upon the announcement by the I.G. that t.i.a.r. the J.W. rises (no ▬{), takes Sp., shows Sn. of F.C., and reports to the W.M. Upon receiving reply the J.W. should dis. Sn. smartly,

* In all cases, when reporting to the W.M., the J.W. should remember not to turn his *body* towards the E. The J.W. should stand square to the N., turning *only his head* towards the W.M. when he addresses him.

keeping both h.'s *open*, resume seat, and give necessary directions to I.G.

2.—During first examination of the Can. the J.W. should remain seated until the reply 'I have.' He then rises, takes Sp., and receives the G. or T. of an E.A.F.M. The J.W. should *not* give the G. or T. until it has first been given by the Can. At conclusion of examination J.W. says, 'Pass . . . .' and resumes seat.

3.—At the next examination, when the Can. is taken to the J.W. after he has been entrusted with the Ss. of the Degree by the W.M., the J.W. remains seated while he directs Can. to adv. to him as a F.C., rising at the answer 'I have.' J.W. takes Sp. and proceeds with the examination. J.W. should *not* give the G. or T. until it has first been given by the Can. At the conclusion of examination J.W. says, 'Pass . . . . . .' and resumes seat.

4.—At the conclusion of the Explanation of the T.B., when the W.M. alludes to a certain symbol the I.P.M. gives —❙, which should be answered by the S.W. and J.W. in proper order.*

THE CEREMONY OF RAISING

1.—Upon the I.G.'s announcement that t.i.a.r., the J.W. rises (no —❙), takes Sp., shows P.Sn., and reports to the W.M. Upon receiving the W.M.'s reply J.W. should dis. Sn. smartly, keeping the hand

* All Brethren should be *standing* during the Explanation of the T.B., the Officers at their correct stations and the rest of the Brethren gathered around the T.B. At the words ' denoting G. the G.G.O.T.U ' (not before), all the Brethren show Sn. of R.

open, and *not forgetting to recover*. He then resumes seat and gives necessary instruction to I.G.

2.—During his examination of the Can. the J.W. should remain seated until the answer 'I have.' He then rises, takes Sp., and receives the G. or T. of an E.A.F.M. The J.W. should *not* give the G. or T. until it has first been given by Can. At conclusion of examination J.W. says, 'Pass . . . .' and resumes seat.

3.—When the Wardens are summoned to assist the W.M. the J.W. leaves his ped. by the left-hand side and proceeds to correct position on right of Can., *not forgetting to take the P.R. with him*. J.W. should direct Can. in a whisper to c.h.f. Hold Can. securely and at proper moment touch his r.t. lightly with P.R.

4.—Be careful to support Can. after W.M.'s words 's.h.a.v.b.o.t.f.' Accidents *have* been known to occur at this stage. After this duty J.W. retires to position behind Can.

5.—When called upon by the W.M. to endeavour to r.t.r.o.o.M.b.t.E.A.'s g..p. the J.W. should advance a few paces and step across Can.'s k...s with r.f. Raise Can.'s r.h. to try the G. Then replace Can.'s r.h. gently by his side * and return direct to former position. J.W. should *not walk backwards*. J.W. takes Sp., shows P.Sn., and reports to W.M. Then dis. Sn. smartly, *not forgetting the recovery*.

6.—Assist W.M. when called upon for a certain duty, and return to seat when directed to do so by the W.M., not before.

* Wardens should note that the Can.'s h.'s should be by his sides and *not* c. on his b. as is sometimes seen.

CALLING OFF AND ON

Every Junior Warden should be thoroughly conversant with the procedure for Calling the Brethren from Labour to Refreshment and *vice versa*. (NOTE.—For details as to this portion of the ceremonial see Chapter XXVII, p. 239.)

CHAPTER XXIV

THE SENIOR WARDEN

BROTHER SENIOR WARDEN in the West is representative of Hiram, King of Tyre, and his column, that of the Doric Order, is typical of Strength. While the Lodge is open this column should be vertical; when the Lodge is Closed, or called from Labour to Refreshment, it should be horizontal.

The Senior Warden is next in rank and power to the Worshipful Master himself, and in the Master's absence he may be required to accept responsibility for the proceedings, although no Warden, not being an Installed Master, may actually occupy the Chair of K.S. In the event of the death or incapacity of the Master, the *Book of Constitutions* (Rule 141) states that it is the Senior Warden who 'shall act as Master' in summoning the Lodge; he would be responsible, through the Secretary, for issuing the Lodge Summons. The *Constitutions* are almost silent as to further powers possessed by this Officer in such an emergency. There seems little doubt, however, that in the event of the death or incapacity of the Master it *must* be the Senior Warden, as the second Officer of the Lodge, who *rules* the Lodge in every respect, with the single exception that (unless already an I.M.) he may not occupy the Master's Chair. In the circumstances referred to it would be his right and his duty to preside at any Committee of the Lodge. Varying opinions are held on this question. The Senior Warden, however, is second in *rank and authority* to the Master himself. In the Master's absence it seems an obvious inference that his authority *must* devolve upon his 'second in command.'

It is thus seen that strength of character and the ability to rule firmly are desirable qualifications for Brother Senior Warden to possess; yet he will be wise to bear in mind that, in all his dealings with his Brethren, strength and firmness gain added dignity and win increasing regard when combined with gentleness and courtesy.

Perhaps the most stimulating reminder which the Senior Warden can receive as to the importance of his Office is the recollection that to him is entrusted the solemn duty of investing the newly made Mason with the distinguishing badge of the Order, the Badge of Innocence and Bond of Friendship.

It might here be noted that to speak of the plain, white apron as the badge of an Entered Apprentice *only* is incorrect; it is the badge of *every* Mason, be he Entered Apprentice or a distinguished Officer of Grand Lodge. Whatever decoration may have been *added* to the apron, beneath it all is to be found the plain, white lambskin, the Symbol of Innocence.

As in the case of our Brother the Junior Warden, we may assume that Brother Senior Warden is already familiar with his duties so far as they apply to the Opening and Closing of the Lodge in the different Degrees. We therefore content ourselves with appending guiding hints relating to the three Ceremonies.

THE CEREMONY OF INITIATION

1.—During his first examination of the Can. the S.W. should remain seated until the J.D. has replied 'By t.h.o.G.b.f.a.o.g.r.' S.W. then rises, takes Can.'s r.h., and says, 'Enter, f.a.o.g.r.' The S.W. should *remain standing* while J.D. places Can. in proper position. S.W. then takes Can.'s r.h. in his own l.h., takes Sp., shows P.Sn. of E.A., and presents the Can. to the W.M.* The S.W. should take the trouble to memorise the full name of the Can., and not have need to consult a copy of the Summons. It is such apparently trifling points which make all the difference between smart and slovenly work.

2.—Upon receiving reply from the W.M. the S.W. should dis. Sn. smartly, keeping the hand *open*, restore Can. to charge of the J.D., and resume seat.

3.—The S.W. *remains seated* when next addressed by the W.M. and told to give the J.D. certain directions.

4.—At the point where the Can. is restored to

* The S.W. must remember that at this stage of the Ceremony in the First Degree the Can. is ' *Mr*,' not ' *Brother* ' as in the subsequent Degrees. (See Chapter X, p. 100, under " The Inner Guard.")

L...t the Wardens should *not* use —⊣. Their action here should be similar to that of the rest of the Brethren.

5.—During the examination of the Can. after he has been entrusted by the W.M. with the Ss. of the Degree the S.W. remains seated until the Can. has answered that he has something to communicate. S.W. should then rise, take Sp., and proceed with examination. The S.W. should *not* give the G. or T. until it has first been given by Can. S.W. remains standing, and shows Sn. of E.A. when presenting Can. to the W.M. for 'some mark . . . .' * Dis. Sn. smartly when W.M. replies, keeping the hand *open*.

6.—Investiture of the Can. with the Badge. The importance of this duty has already been alluded to. S.W. *should not begin his remarks to Can. until the badge is in position.* He should then hold lower right-hand corner of the badge in his l.h. while speaking. Needless to say, the S.W. should be letter-perfect and the words should be spoken with solemn impressiveness. At the words, '. . . never disgrace that Badge . . .' the S.W. strikes badge with his r.h.† S.W. restores Can. to charge of J.D. and resumes his seat. The S.W. should *never leave his ped.* to invest the Can. in any Degree.

* In all cases when presenting a Can. to the W.M. the S.W. should be careful to avoid holding the Can.'s r.h. too high. The S.W. is frequently seen holding Can.'s r.h. *shoulder high,* an exaggerated attitude which looks awkward.

† There should be no hand-clap by the Brethren at this stage ; each Brother should strike his B.

THE CEREMONY OF PASSING

1.—During his first examination of the Can. the S.W. should remain seated until the answer 'I have.' He then rises, takes Sp., and receives the P.G. and P.W. S.W. should *not* give the P.G. until it has first been given by the Can. After examination S.W. *remains standing* while S.D. places Can. in proper position. S.W. then takes Can.'s r.h. in his own l.h., shows Sn. of F., and presents the Can. to W.M.*

2.—Upon receiving the W.M.'s reply the S.W. should dis. Sn. smartly, keeping the hand *open*, restore Can. to charge of S.D., resume seat, and give S.D. necessary directions.

3.—At the next examination of the Can., after he has been entrusted with the Ss. of the Degree by the W.M., the S.W. should remain seated while he directs the Can. to adv. to him as a F.C. first as an E.A., rising when the Can. answers that he has something to communicate. S.W. then takes Sp., and receives the G. or T. of a F.C.F.M. S.W. should *not* give the G. or T. until it is first given by the Can.; at completion of examination S.W. says 'Pass . . . . .' and *remains standing* while S.D. places Can. in proper position. S.W. then takes Can.'s r.h. in his own l.h., shows Sn. of F., and presents Can. to W.M. for some further mark, etc.* Dis. Sn. smartly when W.M. has replied, keeping the hand *open*. Can. is now invested with the B. of a F.C. S.W. must *not* leave his ped. to discharge

* See footnote * on p. 207.

this duty.* S.W. restores Can. to charge of S.D. and resumes his seat.

4.—At the conclusion of the T.B., when the W.M. alludes to a certain symbol, the I.P.M. gives —⚒, which must be answered by S.W. and J.W. in proper order.†

THE CEREMONY OF RAISING

1.—During his first examination of the Can. the S.W. should remain seated until the answer 'I have.' He then rises, takes Sp., and receives the G. or T. of a F.C.F.M. S.W. should not give the G. or T. until it is first given by Can. S.W. then says 'Pass . . . . . .' and resumes seat.

2.—During the next examination the S.W. again remains seated until the Can. answers 'I have.' S.W. then rises, takes Sp., and receives the P.G. and P.W. The S.W. should *not* give the P.G. until it is first received from the Can. At conclusion of examination S.W. says, 'Pass . . . .' and *remains standing* while S.D. places Can. in proper position. S.W. then takes Can.'s r.h. in his own l.h. and presents him to the W.M., showing P.S. of a M.M.‡

3.—Upon receiving the W.M.'s reply the S.W. should dis. Sn. smartly, keeping the hand *open* and *not forgetting to recover*. S.W. restores Can. to charge of S.D. and resumes seat. He then gives Deacons necessary directions.

4.—When the Wardens are summoned to assist

* S.W. should see that the E.A. badge is *removed* before the F.C. badge is adjusted. A badge of a higher Degree should *never* be adjusted over that of a lower Degree.

† See footnote on p. 201.   ‡ See footnote * on p. 207.

the W.M. the S.W. leaves his ped. by the left-hand side and proceeds to correct position on left of Can., *not forgetting to take the L. with him.* Hold Can. securely and at proper moment touch his l.t. lightly with the L.

5.—S.W. should be careful to support Can. properly at the W.M.'s words 's.h.a.v.b.o.t.f.' Accidents *have* been known to occur at this point. After this duty S.W. retires to position behind Can.

6.—When called upon by the W.M. to 'try the F.C.'s,' the S.W. should advance a few paces and step across Can.'s k...s with his l.f. Raise Can.'s r.h. to try the G. Then replace Can.'s r.h. gently by his side * and return direct to former position. S.W. should *not walk backwards.* S.W. takes Sp. and shows P.Sn. when reporting to W.M.; afterwards dis. Sn. smartly, *not forgetting to recover.*

7.—Assist W.M. when called upon for a certain duty, and return to seat when directed to by W.M., not before.

8.—On the Can.'s return to the Lodge, after he has given correct salutes, the S.W. rises and takes Can.'s r.h. in his own l.h. He then takes Sp., shows P.Sn., and presents the Can. to W.M. for some further mark, etc.†

9.—S.W. should dis. Sn. smartly after receiving W.M.'s reply, keeping the hand *open*, and *not forgetting to recover.* S.W. now invests Can. with the B. of a M.M., taking care to see that the F.C. badge is first removed.‡ Can. is then restored to charge of the S.D., and S.W. resumes his seat.

* See footnote on p. 202.   † See footnote * on p. 207.
‡ See footnote * on p. 209.

CHAPTER XXV

THE IMMEDIATE PAST MASTER

STRICTLY speaking, this brief chapter should find no place in a Manual devoted to Lodge Officers and their duties, for the simple reason that the Immediate Past Master is NOT an Officer of the Lodge. Arguments to the contrary have been advanced long and loudly, but the originators of such arguments have yet to advance a single convincing fact in support of their theory.

To say that Brother Immediate Past Master wears a 'Collar of Office' is quite incorrect. He wears a Past Master's Collar to which is appended *exactly the same emblem as that worn by every Past Master in the Craft*, namely, the 47th proposition of the First Book of Euclid suspended from the Square. The Immediate Past Master is in fact the *Junior Past Master of the Lodge*; no more and no less. The Officers of a Private Lodge are clearly defined in Rule 129, *Book of Constitutions.**

Nevertheless the Immediate Past Master has, by virtue of the fact that he *is* the Junior Past Master of the Lodge, a certain stated position in the Lodge

* See p. 85 for List of Officers.

for one year. His place is at the immediate left of the Master, and Rule 141, *Book of Constitutions*, stipulates that in the absence of the Master it is Brother Immediate Past Master who has the first claim to occupancy of the Chair. The *Book of Constitutions* further stipulates (Rule 227) that if the Master of a Lodge be prevented from attending the meetings of the Board of Benevolence 'the Immediate Past Master may supply his place.'

It is evident, therefore, that under certain circumstances the Immediate Past Master is generally regarded as the representative of the Master in the latter's absence. This fact, however, should not lead him to the mistaken impression that he is all-powerful. Instances have been known where, upon the unfortunate death of the Master, Brother Immediate Past Master has jumped to the erroneous impression that he becomes *ipso jure* the *ruler* of the Lodge, and consequent friction has ensued. Any such blunder on the part of the Immediate Past Master can only arise from culpable ignorance of the *Book of Constitutions*, a copy of which was doubtless presented to him at his Initiation and again at his Installation. A reference to Rule 141, *Book of Constitutions*, will make the matter clear to him.*

The Immediate Past Master sometimes holds the mistaken impression that, when the Master does not

* See Chapter XXIV, p. 204, as to who rules the Lodge in the Master's absence.

himself conduct a Ceremony, it is the I.P.M. who has the first right to act as deputy. *He possesses no such claim.* Rule 141, *Book of Constitutions*, as quoted above, makes it clear that it is the Immediate Past Master who has first claim to occupancy of the Chair *in the Master's absence.* When the Master is *present* he alone has the power to decide which Past Master shall take his place if he temporarily vacates his Chair. Similarly, it is for the Master to say who shall deliver the Charge after the Initiation, or give the Explanation of the T.B. after the Passing, if he does not himself attend to these portions of the Ritual.

As already stated, the station of the Immediate Past Master is at the immediate left of the Master, his accepted duty being to render such assistance as the ruler of the Lodge may from time to time require in the rendering of the Ritual. Obviously the Immediate Past Master should be a competent ritualist; otherwise he cannot possibly afford proper assistance to his chief with a diplomatic 'prompt' when occasion demands.

However expert he may be, let Brother Immediate Past Master remember that he should be 'seen and not heard.' Certainly it is no part of his duty to display his own ability at the cost of revealing the Master's imperfections. Nothing is more disconcerting to the Master and irritating to the Brethren than for the Immediate Past Master to be constantly 'butting in' with totally unnecessary corrections. In a regular Lodge it matters nothing if the Master substitutes a word foreign to the Ritual, or transposes a sentence, so long as the *spirit* of the Ritual is being conveyed to the Candidate.

Unfortunately many Immediate Past Masters seem unable to realise this truth, and, strangely enough, the worst offenders are frequently experienced Preceptors. It should be remembered that there is a wide difference between the functions of a Preceptor in his Lodge of Instruction and those of the Immediate Past Master in a regular Lodge.

During Labour Brother Immediate Past Master's duties include the opening of the V.S.L. when the Lodge is opened in the First Degree, and the correct placing of the Sq. and C.'s in that and subsequent Degrees. He should be careful to see that the V.S.L. is correctly placed *so that the Master can read it*; also that the points of the C.'s are *towards the Master.**

At the closing of the Lodge the Immediate Past Master is entrusted with a brief portion of the Ritual, where he reminds the Brethren that 'nothing now remains but, according to ancient custom, to lock up our Ss. in a safe (not "*and sacred*") repository, uniting in the act F.F.F.' The Immediate Past Master should *not* add the ejaculation 'And may G. preserve the Craft.' It is no part of the Ritual and is quite redundant; the Master or Chaplain has

* See para. 6, p. 234 ; also footnote on p. 235.

already offered pious Prayer that the G.A.O.T.U. will 'preserve the Order.'

The Lodge being closed, a fault frequently committed by the Immediate Past Master is to thrust himself forward to take place in the outgoing procession immediately behind the Master. This is quite incorrect. It has the appearance of discourtesy, although probably arising only from lack of knowledge. The Immediate Past Master not being an Officer of the Lodge, he has no prescribed place as such in the procession. Officers of Grand Lodge should follow the Wardens in proper order, followed by Grand Stewards, Brethren of London Rank and of Provincial and District Grand Rank.* Then come the *Past Masters*, among whom the Immediate Past Master is numbered.

At Refreshment Brother Immediate Past Master again occupies the seat at the left of the Master. In the majority of Lodges custom dictates that the Master 'takes wine' with various Brethren and sections of Brethren during the progress of the banquet. It is the Immediate Past Master (as a general rule) who rises to call upon the Brethren whom the Master may desire to honour. In all probability the Master will leave the selection largely to the Brother on his left, and the Immediate Past Master will be well advised to exercise discretion by a strict limitation of the number of times the Master 'takes wine.' The custom of announc-

* See para. 19, p. 172.

ing that the Worshipful Master will 'take wine with
the Brethren on his right' and subsequently 'with
the Brethren on his left' is one to be deplored,
resulting as it generally does in undignified uproar.
The prandial proceedings following a Lodge meeting should be characterised by that same dignity
and decorum which, it is to be hoped, have marked
the proceedings during the period of Labour.
Brother Immediate Past Master may do much towards preserving that dignity and decorum.

CHAPTER XXVI

THE WORSHIPFUL MASTER

THE Freemason who has received from his Brethren the highest honour they have in their power to confer upon him, that of election to the Chair of K.S., finds himself placed in the East,—the ancient seat of Learning and Wisdom. It is to be hoped, therefore, that he has gathered knowledge and wisdom during his passage through the subordinate Offices; that he is well-skilled in the Noble Science; and that he is able and willing to undertake the management of the work and the government of the Lodge.

Yet, even so, the newly installed Master will probably find that he has still much to learn. To attempt, within the scope of a single chapter, to provide him with all the knowledge he will need, would be to essay the impossible; no more can be attempted than a very brief survey of his *rights* and *responsibilities*, and to emphasise a few important rules for his guidance.

1.—*Master's Obligation.*

Every Master-Elect, before he is placed in the Chair, must take an Ob., pledging himself solemnly to preserve the Landmarks of the Order, to observe the ancient usages, and strictly to enforce them in his Lodge.

2.—*Period of Office.*

No Brother may continue as Master for more than two years in succession, unless by dispensation; but he may again be elected after being out of Office for one year. This regulation does not apply to a Prince of the Blood Royal, but it shall apply to his Deputy if such be appointed.

3.—*Dual Mastership.*

A Brother may not rule as Master of more than one Lodge at the same time, except by dispensation.

4.—*Election and Installation.*

Rule 130, *Book of Constitutions*, which relates to the Election of Master, states: "At the next Regular Meeting the first business after the opening of the Lodge shall be the reading of the Minutes of the preceding meeting, and if they be confirmed so far, at least, as relates to the election of Master, he shall be deemed to be elected, and shall be duly installed in the Chair according to ancient usage."

The wording of this rule is not as explicit as it might be; actually, it is the *election itself* which must be confirmed. The inclusion of this point in the *Constitutions* implies that, on so vitally important a question, Grand Lodge deems that the Brethren should have time for reflection. In the absence of any motion to the contrary, the confirmation of the Minutes signifies the confirmation of the election, but the Minutes, as such, are only to be confirmed or non-confirmed on the score of *accuracy of record*. (See Chapter XIX, p. 179.)

Strictly speaking, then, if the Minutes are an accurate record of the proceedings at the Election Meeting they should be confirmed, and a motion for non-confirmation of the election 'arises out of' the Minutes. Such a motion might quite properly be put forward on the grounds that the election was not conducted in a constitutional manner, or even on the grounds of a change of mind among the Brethren. Yet neither of these reasons would imply that the Secretary had inaccurately recorded the happenings at the previous meeting.

5.—*Master's Right to Rule his Lodge.*

Without doubt every Master has the *right* to *rule* his Lodge, and, in so doing, to exercise his own judgment irrespective of any pressure which may be brought to bear upon him. The wise Master will lend a willing ear to the counsel of Brother Secretary and the Past Masters, and will thus find his path made easier. Yet the time may come when, in some case of difficulty, he finds himself conscientiously unable to fall in with the opinions of his seniors in the Craft. In such an unhappy eventuality it would be not merely his right but his *duty* to rely for guidance upon his own judgment, and to exercise his authority without fear. He may find consolation in the reflection that *none* has the right to dispute that authority.

6.—*Master presides at all Meetings.*

Naturally the Master has the *right* to preside at all meetings of the Lodge during his year of Office, a similar right existing in the case of any meeting of a Committee in connection with the Lodge. No Past Master or body of Past Masters may convene any such Committee without the authority of the Master, and if any such meeting be held it would be irregular and the proceedings void.

7.—*Master's Right to Decide the Work.*

It is unfortunately a fact that many Lodge Secretaries take upon themselves powers with which they have never been vested. Particularly is this so in respect to the Lodge Summons. The Master alone has the *right* to decide what work shall appear upon the Summons, and the time at which the Lodge shall meet.

8.—*Master's Ruling Supreme.*

At all Lodge Meetings the Master's ruling is supreme and cannot be questioned. In case of any illegality the Brethren have the remedy of subsequent appeal to higher authority.

9.—*Master has Casting Vote.*

In the case of an equal vote (with certain exceptions) the Master has the *right* to an extra or casting vote. In Rule 182, *Book of Constitutions*, it is definitely stated that when the votes are equal on any question demanding a majority the Master *shall* give a second or casting vote. The Master is, of course, free to use the casting vote as he may think fit; there is no written law to control him. At the same time there is a strong *unwritten law*. The Master should remember that the intended purpose of the casting vote is not to enable him to force his individual convictions upon his Brethren, but rather to assist the Lodge in the case of a possible deadlock. Generally speaking, it should be exercised to preserve the *status quo ante*, and cases may arise where it is the *duty* of the Master to vote *against* his personal convictions.

Assuming, for instance, that there is a motion before the Lodge to change the By-Laws, and that the Master personally favours the change. The matter is surely of vital importance to *all* the Brethren, and should demand a clear majority. The votes being equal, the Master is incurring a grave responsibility if he uses his powers to force such a change from *personal* inclinations. He would be better advised to use the casting vote *against* his personal inclinations, thus preserving the *status quo ante* until the matter may be further considered before it is brought up again before the Lodge.

10.—*Refusing Admission to Visitors.*

Under Rule 151, *Book of Constitutions*, the Master of every Private Lodge has the *right* to refuse admission to a Visiting Brother, although, be it noted, the *Constitutions* add the proviso: "*Whose presence he has reason to believe will disturb the harmony of the Lodge, or to any visitor of known bad character.*"

11.—*Temporary Exclusion of Members.*

Only ignorance of the *Constitutions* can account for the mistaken impression held in many directions that the Master has the power to call upon a Brother to retire from the Lodge. *He has no such power.*

Rule 209, *Book of Constitutions*, states that if any Brother shall behave in Lodge in such a manner as to disturb the harmony of the Lodge, he shall be formally admonished by the Master; and, if he persists in his irregular conduct, he shall be punished by censure, fine, or exclusion for the remainder of the meeting. But it should be noted that the Master *alone* has no right or power to pronounce sentence on the offender. The rule adds: " . . . *according to the opinion of the majority of the members present.*"

It is obvious, therefore, that in any such unhappy eventuality a motion for the offending Brother's exclusion must be duly made and seconded, and carried by a majority of the *members present*. The italicised words are of vital importance. Assuming that twenty-four Brethren were present, and that there were twelve votes for the motion for exclusion, four votes against, and eight abstentions from voting, the motion would be *lost*. A majority of the Brethren *present* (not merely those voting) would demand at least thirteen votes for the motion. It is worthy of notice, too, that in the case of an equal vote of twelve for and twelve against, the Master would not, as in other cases, have the power of a casting vote, the rule definitely stating that decision depends on a *majority* of the *members* present.

12.—*Permanent Exclusion of Members.*

A Lodge has power *permanently* to exclude a Brother for what it may deem to be 'sufficient cause.' In such a case there must be served upon the Brother whose exclusion is under consideration, not less than seven days previous to the meeting, a notice in writing, together with particulars of the complaint against him, stating the time and place appointed for its consideration, when he may attend and be heard. (Rule 210, *Book of Constitutions.*)

In the case of a resolution for permanent exclusion the *Constitutions* stipulate that the power can only be exercised by a majority of not less than *two-thirds* of the members present. Again abstention from voting would count *against* the motion. Assuming an attendance of forty-five members, with twenty-nine voting for exclusion, three against, and thirteen abstaining, the motion would be *lost*. A two-thirds majority would demand not fewer than *thirty* votes for the exclusion.

13.—*Exclusion and Expulsion.*

It should be noted that there is a vast difference between *exclusion* and *expulsion*. A Brother permanently excluded from a Private Lodge is not debarred from seeking admission to another Lodge. Expulsion, on the other hand, would mean total loss of all Masonic status and privileges. Only the Grand Lodge has power to *expel* a Brother from the Craft.

14.—*Master's Right to Appoint Officers.*

A Master's prerogative which is in some danger of being usurped in some directions is his undoubted *right* to appoint his own Officers, with the exception of the Treasurer and Tyler. The Master's powers in this connection are clearly defined in the *Constitutions*, and none has the slightest authority to dispute them. The Master may, if he so desires, consult the Lodge Committee, but no Committee has any claim to decide the appointments to Office. The present writer knows of at least one prominent Emulation-working Lodge where the Master's prerogative in this connection is invariably usurped. Such a practice can only be regarded as an unwise— even a dangerous—precedent.

15.—*Master has no Power to Remove an Officer.*

The Master has no power to displace any Officer once he has been duly appointed and invested. It is set out in Rule 140, *Book of Constitutions*, that should the Master be dissatisfied with the conduct of any Officer he must lay the cause for complaint before the Lodge at a Regular Meeting, not less than seven days' notice of which must be sent to the Brother complained of. The Officer in question can only be displaced if the complaint be deemed well founded by a *majority of the Brethren present*. (See para. 11.) It is, therefore, quite obvious that, during the Installation Ceremony, the Master has *no power* summarily to dismiss the Officers of the Lodge by the sweeping statement that he declares 'all Offices vacant.' (See para. 4, p. 245.)

16.—*Master should Instal his Successor.*

It is not only the *right* but the *duty* of a Master to conduct the Installation of his successor. Among the majority of London Masons such a reminder may appear superfluous. Yet, even in these enlightened times, there *are* Lodges, more particularly in the distant Provinces, wherein senior Past Masters conduct this important ceremony year in and year out. The author knows of one such Lodge where a grey-bearded veteran is wont to proclaim with much pride that he has installed nearly a score of Masters. That same Brother would probably regard it as a personal affront if it were suggested to him that he should stand aside to permit the outgoing Master to conduct the Ceremony. Such a practice is entirely wrong and is inimical to the interests of the Craft. Provided that the outgoing Master is sufficiently a master of his work (as he should be) it cannot be emphasised too strongly that it is his *right* and his *duty* to set the consummating seal upon his period of Office by Installing his successor in the Chair of K.S. Of this prerogative none has the slightest vestige of a right to seek to deprive him.

17.—*Master's Right to Conduct all Ceremonies.*

The Master has a *right* to conduct every Ceremony appearing on the Agenda during his year of Office, but where the list of ceremonial work is a lengthy one he will be ill-advised to insist upon the right if he is in the position of being able to call upon experienced Past Masters for assistance. There are many Lodges, meeting say four or five times a year, which have the Ceremonies of the Three Degrees on the Agenda at every meeting. For the Master to insist on taking all these twelve or fifteen Ceremonies himself savours of conceit and selfishness. Furthermore, however competent a ritualist

15

the Master may be, or may consider himself to be, such an insistence on his rights will undoubtedly inflict boredom on his Brethren.

When the Master has himself passed the Chair he will be in a position to appreciate the fraternal consideration of the Master who shares his responsibilities with the Past Masters and thus gives them a more active interest in the proceedings. The author vividly remembers an occasion when a well-known Emulation-worker, during his year of Mastership, worked all the Three Degrees *and* the Installation Ceremony *at one meeting.* There is nothing clever in such an exhibition; it merely bores the listeners and conveys the impression that the occupant of the Chair is 'showing off.'

18.—*Master not to Surrender his Collar.*

A recent ruling from the authorities has stipulated that when the Master temporarily vacates his chair in favour of a Past Master he should *not* surrender his collar, but that the deputy for the time being should be properly clothed according to his rank.

So multifarious and complex are the prerogatives of the supreme ruler of the Lodge that the list might be extended *ad libitum*; lack of space, however, prohibits extension. The inquiring Brother, recently installed or about to be installed, will do well to spend a quiet hour or two with the *Book of Constitutions*, a book, one fears, all too frequently thrown carelessly aside, and all too seldom studied.

To attempt to deal adequately with the *responsibilities* of the Master of the Lodge within the space at our disposal is another hopeless task. Yet it may be possible to refer to a few points upon which newly installed Masters may be in some doubt.

19.—*Master Responsible for Custody of Warrant.*

No Lodge, except while acting under dispensation in the Dominions or in foreign parts, can meet without a Warrant of Constitution from the Grand Master. This regulation, however, does not apply to the Lodge of Antiquity, No. 2, nor the Royal Somerset House and Inverness Lodge, No. 4, which act under Time Immemorial Constitutions.

If the Warrant be lost or improperly withheld from those lawfully entitled to hold or use it, or withheld by competent Masonic authority, a Lodge must suspend its meetings until a new Warrant or Warrant of Confirmation has been applied for and granted by the Grand Master, or until the withheld Warrant be restored.

Chief among the *responsibilities* of the Master is the custody of the Lodge Charter or Warrant. To every Master this *vitally important* document is entrusted on the night of his Installation; and one of his last duties is to transfer it to his successor. In some Lodges the Warrant is framed and hung in the Lodge Room; in others it is kept with various paraphernalia in the Lodge-box. The former practice is, perhaps, preferable to the latter, but both are wrong. The Master during his year of Office is the rightful custodian of the Warrant and, as such, he should make himself responsible for its safe keeping.

20.—*Master Responsible for Observance of Laws.*

In Rule 153, *Book of Constitutions*, it is laid down that the Master is responsible for the due observance of the laws by the Lodge over which he presides. Obviously, then, the Master should be thoroughly conversant with the *Constitutions* and with the By-Laws of his own Lodge.

21.—*Candidates should receive By-Laws.*

A *responsibility* of the Master, sometimes neglected, is to see that every Initiate and Joining Member is supplied with a printed copy of the Lodge By-Laws. This presentation of the By-Laws to every Brother becoming a member of the Lodge is not merely a custom, it is a definite rule from the Grand Lodge. (See Rule 163, *Book of Constitutions*.)

22.—*Master's Responsibility for Ballots.*

The Master is, of course, responsible for seeing that every ballot is conducted in a constitutional manner. Except in certain cases of emergency, as set forth in Rule 185, *Book of Constitutions*, no person may be made a Mason unless he has been proposed and seconded in open Lodge at one Regular Meeting, and balloted for 'at the next Regular Meeting.' If a Candidate does not present himself for Initiation within one year after his election, the election is void. An election for a Candidate for Initiation or Joining *must* be by ballot, and no Candidate may be elected if, on the ballot, three negative votes appear against him. The By-Laws of a Lodge, however, may enact that one or two negative votes shall exclude a Candidate.

A collective ballot is quite regular, provided that, if there be a negative vote, each Candidate shall then be balloted for individually.* Ballots for Candidates for Initiation and Joining should be taken separately, the motives governing the voting in each case being quite distinct. When announcing the result of a ballot it is as well for the Master to avoid use of the word 'unanimously,' using 'duly' instead. If the By-Laws of the Lodge enact that two negative votes shall exclude a Candidate, and *one* such vote is recorded, the Candidate is still 'duly' elected. Therefore, if the Master announces that he declares the Candidate 'duly elected' his statement is quite accurate and in compliance with the By-Laws.

23.—*Honorary Members.*

A ballot is not necessary for the election of an Honorary Member; this may be done by a show of hands. In the *Book of Constitutions*, Rule 152 reminds us that a Brother who has ceased to be a subscribing Member of a regular Lodge shall not be permitted to visit any Lodge more than once, but that 'this rule shall not apply to the visits of a Brother to any Lodge in which he has been elected an Honorary Member.'

Election to Honorary Membership gives a Brother no status or privileges outside the Lodge which has so elected him. He may not, as an Honorary Member, hold any Office in the Lodge, nor take part in any vote; nor must he be included in the Returns to Grand Lodge.

Whether an Honorary Member has any right to

* See para. 7, p. 247.

partake of refreshment must, of course, be a matter for the decision of the Lodge. Although signing the Attendance Book as a member, he is virtually a guest, and, as such, it is to be assumed that the Lodge will gladly entertain him at the social board.

24.—*Proposal Forms.*

For many years it has been necessary for all Candidates for Initiation and Joining to fill up a Proposal Form, which must also bear the signatures of the Proposer and Seconder, and be countersigned by the Master after the Candidate's admission. This Form, duly completed, must be handed to the Secretary *before* the proposition is made in open Lodge, and must be read *immediately before the ballot is taken.*

25.—*Intervals between Degrees.*

Rule 195, *Book of Constitutions*, points out that an interval of four clear weeks must elapse between the conferment of Degrees (with certain exceptions in Lodges overseas). No doubt Brother Secretary may be trusted to see that no mistake is made under this law, but in this, as in all other matters, the *responsibility* is the Master's.

26.—*Quorum in Lodge.*

The Master should at all times remember that five members must always be present to form a *quorum* before the Lodge can conduct any Masonic business.

Among other *responsibilities* attaching to the occupancy of the Chair of K.S. may be mentioned the instruction of the subordinate Officers; a conviction as to the entire suitability of prospective Candidates; an absolute punctuality in the opening of all Lodge Meetings; a regular attendance at the Quarterly Communications of Grand Lodge; a strict observance of the Landmarks of the Order at all meetings of the Lodge; a thorough knowledge of the Ritual in all its branches.

Well may the newly installed Master who reads these words open his eyes and ask: Am I *really responsible* for all these matters? He *is* responsible for them and for very many others which cannot here be stated.

Unless he be very unfortunately placed, the Master will have the benefit of the counsel of an experienced Secretary and the willing support and co-operation of Past Masters ever ready to help him so far as lies in their power. But to none can he really delegate his responsibilities. As the ruler of the Lodge the Master is largely responsible for its continued progress and welfare. To quote from the impressive address delivered to him at his Installation—*the Honour, Reputation, and Usefulness of the Lodge will materially depend upon the skill and assiduity with which he manages its concerns, while the happiness of its members will be generally promoted in proportion to the zeal and ability with which he promulgates the genuine principles of the Institution.*

Some detailed hints for the guidance of the newly installed Master are set out in the following chapter.

In conclusion, let it again be urged on every present and prospective Master to familiarise himself with the *Book of Constitutions*. Let him remember, too, that he who would rule successfully must first learn to serve loyally.

CHAPTER XXVII

THE WORSHIPFUL MASTER (*contd.*)

OPENING THE LODGE

1.—It is scarcely necessary to emphasise that the W.M. should be early in his attendance at all meetings; punctuality in the W.M. is something more than a desirable virtue, it is a *bounden duty*. There may be many points upon which the Secretary or some other Officer wishes to consult the W.M. before the Lodge is opened and ample time should be allowed. Possibly some of the Officers may be absent, and the W.M. will probably hold consultation with the D.C. as to suitable deputies. It all takes time. The Master who is always punctual and who makes a point of opening the Lodge at the exact time stated on the Summons will find that his example is infectious.

2.—If an Opening Ode is sung it should be sung *before* the Lodge is opened.

3.—Immediately following the Ode the W.M. gives ▬ to call the Brethren to order and proceeds: 'Brethren, assist me to open the Lodge.' The W.M. should remember when putting the first two questions to the Wardens that he addresses them *by name*. Needless to say, that when the W.M. calls the Brethren to order 'in the First Degree' he should himself set an example of smartness in this connection. All the W.M.'s Sns. should be given with military precision and smartness.

4.—At the Emulation Lodge of Improvement the question as to the Master's place is *always* addressed to the S.W. In the majority of regular Emulation-working Lodges it is addressed to the I.P.M.

5.—Perfect understanding is essential between the W.M. and the Chaplain, if there be a Chaplain among the Officers. In many Lodges the W.M. says, 'The Lodge being duly formed . . .,' and the Chaplain then adds: 'Before the W.M. declares it open let us invoke . . .' It seems a clumsy and unnecessary procedure thus to divide one sentence between two speakers. A better method is for the Chaplain to say: 'The Lodge being duly formed, before the W.M. declares it open . . .' * Where there is no Chaplain (as at Emulation Lodge of Improvement), the W.M., of course, renders this portion of the Ritual.

6.—Upon the words: 'I declare the Lodge duly open,' the W.M. and all Brethren should dis. Sn. smartly, keeping the hand *open*.† The W.M. then gives proper ——. He should *not* be seated until the Tyler has replied to the I.G.'s Ks.‡ The I.P.M. will attend to the opening of the V.S.L. and the

* A similar practice is advisable when Opening the Lodge in the Second Degree, and when Closing in the Second and First Degrees.

† Similarly in the Second and Third Degrees. The hand should be kept open when discharging *all* Masonic Sns.

‡ Similar directions apply when opening or closing the Lodge in all Degrees.

placing of the Sq. and C.'s.   The W.M., however, should be sure that the V.S.L. is correctly placed *so that he can read it.**   The Sq. and C.'s should be so placed that the points of the latter are *towards the W.M.*

OPENING THE LODGE IN THE SECOND DEGREE

7.—Remembering his *responsibilities* the W.M. must be careful to see that any E.A.'s retire before the Lodge is opened in the Second Degree.   Even though he has reason to believe that none is present, it is a wise precaution to use the familiar phrase: 'If there are any E.A.'s present I must now ask them to retire from the Lodge.'   The W.M. can never go wrong in doing this, as a Lodge *cannot* be opened *directly* into the Second or Third Degree.

8.—When discharging the Sn. the W.M. should drop the l.h. at the words 'duly open,' and draw the r.h. smartly a.t.b. at the words 'on the Sq.'

9.—The Lodge being open in the Second Degree the I.P.M. will attend to the Sq. and C.'s.   It does *not* matter which p...t of the C.'s is exposed.

OPENING THE LODGE IN THE THIRD DEGREE

10.—The W.M. should request all F.C.'s to retire before proceeding.

* It is *not* necessary that the V.S.L. should be open at any particular chapter.   The First Great Light in Masonry is the *entire volume.*   It *must* be open while the Lodge is at Labour, but there is no authority for insisting upon opening it at any particular chapter or page.

11.—When discharging the Sn. at the words 'duly open on the C.,' the W.M. should remember that there is *no recovery* at this point. This is the *only occasion* when there is no recovery in discharging the P.Sn. of the Third Degree.*

CLOSING THE LODGE IN THE THIRD DEGREE

12.—There is probably no part of Masonic ceremonial more frequently marred by clumsiness and inexperience than the communication of the Subs. Ss. of a M.M. between the Wardens and between the W.M. and S.W. The proceedings cannot be described here in detail; practice in a L.I. is the only way to attain perfection. It may be mentioned, however, that there is frequently unnecessary delay after the communication of the Subs. Ss. by the S.W. to the W.M. Each waits for the other to move. It is the W.M., as the senior Officer, who should first turn away and return to his seat.†

13.—When the G. or R. Sn. is given at the words 'All G. to the M.H.' the r.h. should be brought back immediately to position for the P.Sn., and *not* first dropped to the side.

14.—After giving Brother S.W. his command to close the Lodge the W.M. should give the K.'s with

---

* In discharging the Sn. the hand should *not* first be moved across to the l. of the b..y. Such a movement is frequently seen, but it is not in accordance with correct Emulation procedure.

† The first stage in communicating the Subs. Ss. of a M.M. is the P.G. and P.W. leading from the Second to the Third Degree. Then follow the Sns. of H. and S. and the P.Sn. Finally the W...s of a M.M. are given on the F.P.O.F. The Sns. of the E.A. and F.C. Degree should *not* be given.

his *left* hand, maintaining the P.Sn. with his r.h. The correct K.'s at this stage are those of the *Third Degree.*

CLOSING THE LODGE IN THE SECOND DEGREE

15.—After giving the S.W. his command to close the Lodge the W.M. should give the K.'s with his *left* hand, immediately elevating it again to resume the H.Sn. or Sn. of P. The correct K.'s at this stage are those of the *Second Degree.**

CLOSING THE LODGE GENERALLY

16.—After giving the S.W. his command to close the Lodge the W.M. should give the K.'s with his *left* hand, maintaining the P.Sn. with his r.h. The correct K.'s at this stage are those of the *First Degree.**

17.—If a Closing Ode is sung, it should be sung *after* the Lodge is Closed.

THE RISINGS

At all Regular Meetings the Master, prior to the Closing of the Lodge, 'rises' for the first, second, and third times to 'ask if any Brother has aught to propose for the good of Freemasonry in general or of this —— Lodge in particular.' This is not so done at an Emergency Meeting, because such a meeting is called for a distinct, emergent purpose, which must be stated on the Summons, and no other business may be transacted.†

* See p. 285.
† See Chapter XIX, p. 179, under 'The Secretary' and para. 6, p. 247.

The Master's correct method of procedure for the 'risings' is to give one ━━▐, which is answered by the Wardens. He then rises for the first time to 'ask if any Brother has aught to propose . . .'

It is impossible to lay down hard and fast rules as to the particular business to be dealt with on each 'rising'; much depends upon local or Lodge customs, and none has any right to dogmatise on the subject. Generally speaking, however, it is a safe rule to reserve the 'first rising' for matters connected with Grand Lodge.*

If there are no Grand Lodge matters to be dealt with it is a common custom for Brother Secretary to rise with Sp. and Sn. and announce: 'Nothing from Grand Lodge, W.M.'

The W.M. then repeats ━━▐ and rises to repeat his question for the second time. Again local and Lodge customs must dictate procedure. In many Provincial Lodges it is customary to reserve this rising for matters connected with the Provincial Grand Lodge, all other business being dealt with on the 'third rising.' If there are no Provincial Grand Lodge matters Brother Secretary rises with Sp. and Sn. and announces: 'Nothing from Provincial Grand Lodge, W.M.'

The business for the 'second rising' duly disposed of, the Master again gives ━━▐ and rises to put his inquiry for the third time, when any other business may be brought before the Lodge.

* It sometimes happens that on this ' rising ' Brother Secretary has to read a communication *from the Grand Master.* If so, Brother D.C. should call the Brethren to Order. The Brethren should always stand to receive a message from the Grand Master.

At Emulation Lodge of Improvement the I.P.M. always rises in his place on the 'third rising,' stands to O. with the Sp. and Sn., and says: 'Hearty Good Wishes, W.M.' This is so done in the recognised Lodges of Instruction, and in many regular Lodges which follow the Emulation system.

In Provincial Lodges it is a common custom on the 'third rising' for Visiting Brethren to rise in turn to tender 'Hearty Good Wishes' from their respective Lodges. It has been widely stated that such procedure is irregular, and a high official connected with the Grand Lodge, a late Grand Registrar, gave it as his opinion that no Brother has the right to convey 'Hearty Good Wishes' from a Lodge unless he is the Master of that particular Lodge, or has been especially authorised by the Master so to do. As a matter of fact, Grand Lodge has given no ruling on the point. The opinion quoted above would seem to be a sound one, but Brethren will do well to be guided by local custom.

CALLING OFF AND ON

For the Ceremony of Calling the Brethren from Labour to Refreshment (or Calling Off, as it is generally known) the W.M. should give one ⚒, which is answered by the Wardens. The W.M. then says: 'Principal Officers upstanding,' when he and his Wardens rise, the rest of the Brethren remaining seated. The W.M. then asks: 'Bro. J.W., what time is it?' to which the J.W. replies: 'High time, W.M.' The W.M. asks: 'Your duty?' to which J.W. answers: 'To call the

Brethren from Labour to Refreshment.' The
W.M. says: 'I will thank you to declare it.' J.W.
then announces: 'Brethren, it is the W.M.'s
command that you cease Labour and go to Refreshment; keep within hail so as to come on in due time,
that profit and pleasure may be the result.'

The J.W. gives one ⎯▮, which is answered first
by the S.W. and then by the W.M. The I.P.M.
should close the V.S.L. without moving the S. and
C.'s. The J.W. raises his column and the S.W.
lowers his column. In many Lodges it is customary
for the J.D. to turn the T.B. over at this point, but
there is no precedent for such procedure according
to strict Emulation-working, as the T.B. is *not*
changed for the openings and closings in the
different degrees at Emulation Lodge of Improvement.

The Brethren being assembled in Lodge for the
Call from Refreshment to Labour (or Calling On),
the W.M. gives one ⎯▮, which is answered by the
Wardens. W.M. says: 'Principal Officers upstanding,' when he and his Wardens rise, the rest
of the Brethren remaining seated. The W.M.
asks: 'Bro. J.W. what time is it?' to which the
J.W. replies: 'Past High time, W.M.' The W.M.
asks: 'Your duty?' and the J.W. answers: 'To call
the Brethren from Refreshment to Labour.' The
W.M. says: 'I will thank you to declare it.' The
J.W. then announces: 'Brethren, it is the W.M.'s
command that you cease Refreshment and return
to Labour, for the further despatch of Masonic
business.'

The J.W. gives ⎯▮ and lowers his column.

S.W. then gives ━◣ and raises his column. The W.M. then gives ━◣. The I.P.M. opens the V.S.L. If the T.B. has previously been reversed, the J.D. attends to it.

RESUMING THE LODGE

The correct procedure for Resuming the Lodge is as follows: The W.M. gives single ━◣, which is answered by the Wardens. The W.M. then announces: 'Brethren, by virtue of the power in me vested, I resume the Lodge in the . . . Degree.' He then gives ━◣ *of the Degree into which the Lodge is resumed.* The Wardens give similar ━◣. The I.G. proceeds to the door and gives similar K.'s, to which the Tyler replies. I.P.M. adjusts the Sq. and C.'s, and the J.D. attends to the T.B. (NOTE.—See footnote to Appendix B, pp. 285, 286, with regard to 'muffled' K.'s.)

THE CEREMONIES

To tabulate details for the Master's guidance in all the Ceremonies would require far more space than the writer has at his command. Perfection can only come from careful study of the Ritual combined with diligent practice in a reliable Lodge of Instruction.* The few hints hereunder set out, however, will be of assistance.

* See p. 283 for List of Recognised Emulation-working Lodges of Instruction.

16

THE CEREMONY OF INITIATION

1.—Prior to the Ob. the W.M. should exercise *great care* in adjusting one p...t of the C.'s to the Can.'s n.l.b.

2.—The correct Sn. during the Ob. is the P.Sn. of the Degree.

3.—When making a certain movement during the Ob. at the words 'hereby and hereon' the W.M. should use his l.h., maintaining the P.Sn. with his r.h. The word 'hele' is pronounced 'HAIL.' *

4.—The correct point at which to dis. Sn. is immediately the Can. has repeated the final words of the Ob.† The W.M. should remember to remove the C.'s at this point.

5.—Restoration to L...t. The importance of this portion of the Ceremony has been stressed in Chapter XVI, para. 8, p. 134, *q.v.* Perfect understanding between the W.M. and J.D. is essential. The W.M. should hold his g.v.l aloft so that all may see it. Three distinct and deliberate movements should be made, *i.e.* across to the left, across to the right, then down, the J.D. removing the h.-w. as the W.M.'s g.v.l descends in the final movement.

6.—When rising to communicate the Ss. of the Degree to the Can. the W.M. should remember to take the Sp. When communicating the G. or T. to the Can. at this point it is the W.M. and *not the J.D.* who adjusts the Can.'s t...b.‡ (See footnote, p. 134.)

* These directions apply to all Degrees.
† This direction applies to all Degrees.
‡ This direction applies also at similar stage in the Second Degree.

7.—Explanation of the W.T.'s. Unless the W.M. be an expert ritualist it were better *not to handle the W.T.'s.* The mere fact of doing so is often sufficient to cause a lapse of memory. The W.M. does *not stand to explain the W.T.'s.**

8.—The Charge after Initiation. If the Charge is delivered by the W.M. he *does not stand* for this duty.

THE CEREMONY OF PASSING

1.—The correct Sn. during the Ob. in this Degree is the Sn. of F. The W.M. should use his *left* hand for a certain movement at the words 'hereby and hereon,' maintaining Sn. of F. with r.h. The Sn. should be discharged when the Can. repeats the final words of the Ob.

2.—The W.M. should remember to take the Sp. when rising to communicate the Ss. of the Degree to the Can.

3.—The W.M. does not stand for the explanation of the W.T.'s. (See para. 7 above.)

4.—Explanation of the T.B. Upon the Can.'s return to the Lodge the W.M. should wait until he has been saluted and the S.D. has placed the Can. in correct position at the foot of the T.B. The W.M. then leaves his ped. on the left-hand side and proceeds to the head of the T.B., where J.D. will hand him his wand to point out the emblems.†

* These directions apply to all Degrees.
† See footnote on p. 201.

THE CEREMONY OF RAISING

1.—The correct Sn. during the Ob. is the P.Sn. of the Degree. The W.M. should use his *left* hand for a certain movement at the words 'hereby and hereon,' maintaining the P.Sn. with r.h. The correct moment to dis. Sn. is when Can. repeats final words of the Ob. *Do not forget to recover.*

2.—At the words 'Rise newly Ob. M.M.,' the W.M. should use the *right hand only*.

3.—At the words, 'when the villain who was a.w.a.h.m.s.h.a.v.b.o.t.f.,' the W.M. should make a motion with the M..l. He should *not* leave his seat to touch Can.'s F......d with the M..l.

4.—The W.M. should remember that the Can. ought to be r..s.d on the F.P.O.F. Practice is essential before this can be done correctly.

5.—Following the concluding words of the Charge—'peace and salvation to the faithful and obedient of the human race'—the W.M. takes both the Can.'s h.'s in his own and moves slowly round to the right until they occupy each other's places, the W.M. facing the S. and the Can. facing N. Even among experienced Preceptors there is often a doubt as to the correct direction of this movement. No mistake can be made if the W.M. remembers that the movement should be made in an *anticlockwise* direction.

6.—During the T.H. the W.M. should *not* take Sp. when he rises at the words 'one of the Brethren, looking round, observed . . .'

7.—Later, when the W.M. rises to demonstrate the five Sns., then he should take the Sp.

THE CEREMONY OF INSTALLATION

1.—When signifying his assent with the Sn. of F. to the Ancient Charges and Regulations read by the Secretary, the M.-E. should remember that the Sn. is *dropped*, not drawn.

2.—When directed to advance to the ped. to take the S. Ob. of M.-E., the M.-E. should *not* advance until the I.M. has *completed his sentence*.

3.—The correct Sn. during the Ob. is the Sn. of F. The Sn. should be discharged when the M.-E. repeats final words of the Ob.

4.—The W.M. should *not* 'declare all Offices vacant' at any period during this Ceremony. A reference to Rule 140, *Book of Constitutions*, will show the only method by which a Master is empowered to displace an Officer. Under the *Constitutions* no Master of a Lodge has the power simultaneously to displace all the officers by a mere declaration that all Offices are vacant.*

5.—The I.W. For obvious reasons detailed hints cannot here be set down regarding this important portion of the Ceremony. The I.M., however, should remember that there should be *no movement to illustrate the words* when he refers to the p...lty at the end of the Ob. The correct word here is 'slung,' *not* 'flung' as is so often heard. The meaning of the sentence is that the h. shall be *slung* over the l.s.—*i.e.* suspended in a sling for all to see as a visible mark of degradation.

6.—When the Brethren are readmitted and

* See footnote, p. 171 and para. 15, p. 224.

directed to pass round the Lodge and salute the W.M., they should not be told to do so 'in passing.'*

7.—The W.T.'s of each Degree should be explained *in extenso* by the I.M. If, however, the W.T.'s of any Degree have already been explained during the course of the meeting it is sufficient for the I.M. to say: "Their uses and significations having already been explained this evening, I will not take up your time with a repetition."

8.—The Lodge should be *fully Closed in all Degrees.*

9.—The Address to the newly installed Master at the conclusion of the Ceremony should be given from the W. at the left of the S.W. The Addresses to the Wardens and Brethren should *both* be given from the E., at the left of the W.M. Neither the W.M. nor the Wardens should stand when being addressed.

GENERAL HINTS (DURING LABOUR)

1.—The W.M.'s first duty is to see that the Warrant is in evidence.†

2.—In the event of a visit by the Grand Master, the Pro Grand Master, or the Deputy Grand Master (or, in a Provincial or District Lodge, by the Provincial or District Grand Master or his Deputy or Assistant), the W.M. of a Private Lodge *must* tender his gavel to the distinguished visitor, but *to no other Grand Officer however elevated in rank.*

* See footnote on p. 146.
† See Chapter XXVI, para. 19, p. 227.

3.—A copy of the *Book of Constitutions* and of the Lodge By-Laws should *always* be presented to each Initiate.*

4.—If Minutes of more than one Meeting have to be read they should be put for confirmation *separately*. The Master should not declare the Minutes to be *carried*. A resolution is 'carried,' but Minutes are *confirmed*.

5.—If any of the proceedings at a Lodge Meeting necessitate the procuring of a Dispensation, such Dispensation *must* be read in Open Lodge before the particular business is entered upon. In the case of a Lodge actually meeting by Dispensation it is customary for the Dispensation to be read immediately after the opening of the Lodge. It is *not correct* for the Dispensation to be read *before* the Lodge is opened. The meeting is legalised not by the *reading* of the Dispensation but by the fact that it *has been procured*.

6.—The W.M. may summon a Lodge of Emergency at any time, for which no Dispensation is necessary. No other business save that stated on the Summons may be entered upon at an Emergency Meeting.† Minutes are *not* read and the W.M. does *not* rise to inquire ' if any Brother has aught to propose . . .'

7.—A collective ballot for more than one Candidate for Initiation is permissible; similarly for Candidates for Joining. But ballots for Candidates for Initiation and Joining should be taken separately.

* See Chapter XXVI, para. 21, p. 228.
† See Chapter XIX, p. 179, under ' The Secretary,' and p. 237 under ' The Risings.'

The W.M. should be careful to assure himself that the 'Nay' drawer is empty before the ballot-box is circulated.*

8.—In the case of any awkward situation arising the W.M. has the power to suspend the proceedings by the simple expedient of Calling the Lodge from Labour to Refreshment. Difficult situations have sometimes been overcome by adopting this course. Every Master and J.W. should be familiar with the Ceremony of Calling Off and Calling On.†

9.—No nominations are permissible for the Offices of Master and Treasurer. These officers *must* be elected by *free ballot*. The Tyler may be elected by a show of hands.

GENERAL HINTS (DURING REFRESHMENT)

10.—The W.M. should remember that punctuality is almost as important in terminating the proceedings of the evening as in commencing them. It is a wise procedure to draft a time-table—*and keep to it!* Custom dictates that certain toasts should be honoured, however much we might like to dispense with them. A lengthy musical programme is generally a nuisance. It is better to cut down the musical programme than for late speakers to be compelled to address empty seats.

11.—Smoking must not be permitted until after the toasts of 'The King' and 'The M.W. the Grand Master.' This stipulation, however, does *not* apply to the cigarette served with the sorbet. If

* See Chapter XXVI, para. 22, p. 228.   † See p. 239.

a sorbet is served the W.M. should *not give the loyal toast at this stage*. Such a custom is a modern innovation as inconsistent as it is unauthorised. If a mid-prandial cigarette is permitted the W.M. should see that it is not lighted *before* the sorbet is served, nor continued *after* that course is completed.*

12.—If the custom of the Lodge dictates that the W.M. should 'take wine' with various Brethren during the banquet, he should *always stand* to do so. Ordinary courtesy *demands* it, the W.M. being in the capacity of host at the dinner-table. Politeness also dictates that the Brother, or Brethren, with whom the Master is 'taking wine' should stand. The very modern practice, when the Master is 'taking wine' with 'All the Brethren,' for the toastmaster to announce: 'The Brethren will remain seated,' is to be regretted. Common courtesy surely demands that the Brethren should rise to acknowledge the Master's hospitable greeting.

13.—It is not customary for Grand Officers to rise when the Master 'takes wine' with 'The Visitors.' Possibly the explanation is that these eminent Brethren, having already been greeted by the Master, should not be 'inconvenienced' a second time; but it is quite inaccurate to argue that a Grand Officer is *not* a visitor. One sometimes hears ingenious Brethren endeavour to explain that, while 'ordinary' Brethren are 'visitors,' Grand Officers are 'guests'—a distinction *without* a difference.† The truth is, of course, that a visiting Grand Officer at the dinner-table is in *exactly the*

---

* See Chapter XXIX. † See footnote on p. 99.

same position as any other visiting Brother; he is a guest being entertained by the Lodge. Save that his rank ordains that he has a particular seat allotted to him, and that he receives certain formal honours, his privileges as a guest are the same as those of the youngest visiting Entered Apprentice, no more and no less.

14.—The custom of 'toasting' or 'challenging' among the Brethren during the dinner is frequently carried to excess, with the result that an undignified 'bear-garden' atmosphere prevails. It is the duty of the W.M. to exert his authority to insure that there shall not be unseemly noise. Strict etiquette demands that no Brother shall 'challenge' one of senior rank. Consequently the W.M. may *never* be 'challenged.' The Board of General Purposes has called attention to the regrettable habit of constantly 'challenging' the Initiate. The W.M. should not permit anything of the sort. The W.M. will be wise if he does *not* let it be announced that he desires visiting Brethren to 'make themselves at home' by joining in the 'challenging.' In all probability there will be quite enough noise while the practice is limited to members of the Lodge.

15.—The W.M. should *not* permit Brother Organist to introduce a paid artiste into the room to sing the National Anthem as a solo. The National Anthem *is* an anthem, and, as such, it should be rendered by the Brethren as a whole.

16.—Every W.M. should exercise the most careful supervision over the musical programme. No item of a questionable or suggestive nature should *ever* be permitted in a Masonic atmosphere. Nor, of course, should any Brother ever be permitted to tell a story of such a nature. Unfortunately such a thing sometimes happens, and the Master who immediately exercises his authority will certainly earn the respect and support of the Brethren.

17.—Topics likely to give rise to argument or vexation are better omitted from post-prandial speeches. A spirit of harmony and fraternity should prevail during the period of Refreshment; it should never be permitted to assume the nature of a debate.

PART III
MISCELLANEOUS MATTERS

PART III

MISCELLANEOUS MATTERS

CHAPTER XXVIII

THE LODGE OF INSTRUCTION *

RULES 158–161, *Book of Constitutions*, state the procedure under which a Lodge of Instruction may be held, but the guidance contained therein is necessarily very brief. Rule 158 stipulates that no Lodge of Instruction shall be held unless under the sanction of a regular, warranted Lodge, or by special licence and authority of the Grand Master. Further, that the Lodge giving its sanction, and the Brethren to whom the licence is granted, shall be answerable for the proceedings, and responsible that the mode of working adopted *has received the sanction of the Grand Lodge*. Rule 159 reminds us that notice of the times and places of meeting must be submitted to the Grand Secretary (or, in Provinces and Districts, to the Provincial or District Grand Secretary), and in Rule 160 it is laid down that Lodges of Instruction must keep Minutes recording the names of all Brethren present and of

* See Appendix A, p. 283, for List of Recognised Lodges of Instruction.

Brethren appointed to hold office. In Rule 161 reference is made to the fact that a regular Lodge may at will withdraw sanction from its Lodge of Instruction. Not much helpful material here for the use of Brethren seeking guidance as to the formation and control of a Lodge of Instruction.

Obviously the first concern of a group of Brethren desirous of forming a Lodge of Instruction is, in compliance with Rule 158, *Book of Constitutions*, to assure themselves that they can obtain the sanction of a regular Lodge. No actual warrant is necessary, the *Constitutions* are complied with by a recording of the sanctioning Lodge's permission in the Lodge Minute Book. It is usual for such permission to be conveyed in a letter from the Secretary of the regular Lodge to the Secretary of the proposed Lodge of Instruction, and such letter (or a copy thereof) may be framed, mounted, or otherwise preserved for use as the 'Warrant' of the Lodge of Instruction.

Even before this important matter is disposed of, the would-be Founders of the suggested Lodge of Instruction will doubtless have given careful consideration to other questions of equal importance. It seems scarcely necessary to emphasise that there should be absolute unanimity as to the particular mode of working to be taught; and, the decision arrived at, it should be rigidly adhered to. Nothing can be more detrimental to the harmonious and successful conduct of a Lodge of Instruction than for different Brethren to endeavour to introduce varying systems of working. Any such practice, if permitted, will inevitably result in chaos, and 'profit and pleasure' will certainly be conspicuous by their absence.

The selection of a competent Preceptor is obviously a matter of paramount importance. Having elected their Preceptor, the Brethren should give him their complete confidence and at all times accept his ruling without question or resentment; his very title signifies that from him they take their law. As in the Regular Lodge the Master is the pre-eminent authority, so in the Lodge of Instruction the Preceptor's word should be the law on all matters. If the Brethren find his law unacceptable, then their only proper course is to elect another Preceptor, or to seek instruction elsewhere.

The qualifications which contribute to the making of a successful Preceptor are many and varied. It goes without saying that he must be a master of the ritual in all its branches, but much more is required of him than a comprehensive knowledge of the different Ceremonies and Lectures. The Preceptor who is to obtain and retain the confidence of his pupils must possess the natural gift of leadership; he must at all times be able to command, but the commanding should be combined with a quiet courtesy of demeanour, a pleasantness of manner which will take the 'sting' out of the many corrections he will be called upon to make.

17

Brother Preceptor, if he wins the confidence of his pupils, will undoubtedly be consulted on multifarious points beyond the actual working of the Ceremonies; he will be looked up to as a reliable 'authority.' He should, therefore, be thoroughly acquainted with Masonic etiquette, jurisprudence, and history. Above all, he *must* possess the all too rare ability to impart his knowledge to others. Comparison has been made between the Master of a Lodge and the Preceptor of a Lodge of Instruction; it may be added that the Preceptor's powers and responsibilities are even greater than those of a Master.

The Officer next in importance to the Preceptor in a Lodge of Instruction is the Secretary. While he need not necessarily possess his colleague's mastery of ritual, he should, if he is to discharge his duties efficiently, be a past master in other directions. He must be an expert organiser, courteous and patient in his dealings with sometimes troublesome Brethren, and, beyond all else, a tireless and willing worker. The meetings being held at frequent intervals, generally weekly, the secretarial duties appertaining to a Lodge of Instruction are far greater than in a Regular Lodge. In the happy and successful Lodge of Instruction the Preceptor and Secretary should at all times work in complete accord, but Brother Secretary should remember that the Preceptor *is* the Preceptor, and as such, the paramount authority.

The Preceptor and Secretary are assisted by a Committee, and there is wisdom in limiting the number of members elected to the Committee; a large Committee is unnecessary and may well prove more of a hindrance than a help. In the recognised Emulation-working Lodges of Instruction election to the Committee pre-supposes that the Brother elected is sufficiently expert at the ritual to be of practical assistance to the Preceptor, and to act as his deputy in his absence if called upon.

However expert a Preceptor may be, precepting is always more than a one-man job. The Preceptor will, of course, be following the Master's work carefully, but he must be equally attentive to the other Officers; his attention must be here, there, and everywhere. With it all he is, after all, only human, and his brain *is* a human brain and not an infallible machine; an occasional moment of uncertainty is inevitable, and, when that moment comes, it is the Committee-man seated on the Preceptor's immediate left who should be ready and competent to render the necessary assistance promptly and unobtrusively. Smooth team-work should characterise the Committee's efforts in every well-conducted Lodge of Instruction, and nowhere is such efficient team-work more strongly in evidence than in the Emulation Lodge of Improvement and the recognised Emulation-working Lodges of Instruction.

In a Lodge of Instruction which hopes for a long

and successful career all the proceedings should be conducted with as much regularity and formality as in a Regular Lodge. As already mentioned, the *Constitutions* stipulate that the Secretary must keep proper Minutes of the proceedings, and the *Constitutions* further ordain that such Minutes must be produced if called for by the Grand Master or his deputies, or by the Lodge granting its sanction.

Rule 160, *Book of Constitutions*, not only directs that a Lodge of Instruction shall keep proper Minutes, it adds that the Minutes shall record the names of all Brethren appointed to hold Office. The election of Master and the appointment of Officers for an ensuing meeting are matters which should always be conducted with proper formality.

In the recognised Lodges of Instruction the election of Master always takes place on the Second Rising. The procedure is as follows: The W.M. rises for the second time to 'ask if any Brother has aught to propose . . .' whereupon the Preceptor (or any deputy who may be acting as I.P.M.) rises with Sp. and Sn. and says: 'W.M., I have pleasure in proposing (or 'I beg to propose') that Bro. S.W. occupy (or 'take') the chair at our next meeting.' Another Member of the Committee rises with Sp. and Sn. and says: 'W.M., I have pleasure in seconding (or 'I beg to second') the proposition.' The W.M. (no ⎯⬗) says: 'Brethren, you have heard the proposition.* All those in favour will signify in the manner usually observed among Masons.' (The Brethren signify.) 'On the contrary?'

The W.M. then announces: 'Bro. S.W. (S.W. rises at once with Sp. and Sn.),† you have been unanimously elected to occupy this chair on ...day evening next. You will appoint *your* Officers and name *the* work.' The S.W. replies: 'W.M. and Brethren, I thank you.' He then discharges Sn., resumes his seat, and appoints his Officers, or says: 'The Officers will follow in rotation, and the work will be the . . . Ceremony and . . .' The Officers are *always* appointed at Emulation Lodge of Improvement. The procedure is for the S.W. to say: 'Bro. J.W. (J.W. rises with Sp. and Sn.), will you occupy this chair on ...day evening next?' The J.W. answers: 'With pleasure, Bro. Master-Elect,' then discharges Sn. and resumes his seat. The S.W. says: 'Bro. S.D. (S.D. rises with Sp. and Sn.), will you occupy the J.W.'s chair?' S.D. replies as above, discharges Sn., and resumes his seat. S.W. proceeds: 'Bro. J.D. (J.D. rises with

* It is quite superfluous for the Master to say : ' Brethren, it has been proposed by Bro. A., and seconded by Bro. B., that Bro. S.W. be elected,' etc., etc. The Brethren have heard the proposition ; there is no need to repeat it.

† Here is an apparent exception to the ruling given in Chapter VII, pp. 76 and 77, where it is stated that according to Emulation practice a junior does *not* stand to O. when addressed by a senior Officer. But it must be borne in mind that the ruling there given refers to Emulation practice *only during the actual Ceremonies.*

Sp. and Sn.), will you *act* as S.D.?' Similar procedure with remaining Officers.

The procedure for announcing the Ceremony for rehearsal is as follows: The W.M. (no ⟼) announces: 'Brethren, the Ceremony for rehearsal this evening is that of . . . and Bro. A.B. will act as Candidate' (or 'I will thank some Brother to offer himself as Candidate'). The Brethren who rise to offer themselves should *not* show Sn. If the Ceremony named is that of Initiation, the Brother selected as Candidate proceeds to the left of the S.W., salutes the W.M., and retires to be p.p. If the Ceremony for rehearsal be that of Passing or Raising, the selected Candidate remains standing in his place, and the J.D. or S.D. (according to the Ceremony) should fetch him and conduct him to the left of the S.W. There is *no salute* here prior to the Master proceeding: 'Brethren, Bro. A.B. is this evening a Candidate to be . . .'

In a Lodge of Instruction the First Rising should be for propositions for new Members, the Second Rising for the election of Master for the ensuing meeting, and the Third Rising for other business. Of course, if there *should* be any communication from Grand Lodge to be read, it will be taken on the First Rising as in a regular Lodge.

The nearer the 'atmosphere' of the Lodge of Instruction approximates to that of a Regular Lodge, the keener will be the attention of the Brethren and the smarter the work. The question of furnishing is, therefore, one of considerable importance; the furniture, working-tools, and other appointments should be as complete as possible. This necessarily entails a rather heavy initial outlay and possibly some sacrifice on the part of the Founders, but the certain results are well worth the cost. All *Officers* at a Lodge of Instruction should wear Masonic clothing, aprons and collars being provided from the funds for that purpose. Other Brethren may reasonably be excused from wearing Masonic clothing.

The question of a suitable meeting-place for a Lodge of Instruction is a difficult one, and the difficulty becomes more pronounced each year with the continued expansion of the Craft. In this connection Brethren in the Provinces are, in the majority of cases, more fortunately placed than those in the Metropolitan area. Many Provincial Lodges of Instruction are able to meet in their local Masonic Halls, often in the same room in which they hold their Regular Lodges.

In London most Lodges of Instruction can find accommodation only on licensed premises, the use of the room being granted for a nominal sum by the licensee, who expects (perhaps not unnaturally) to attract trade. Where such conditions obtain, the Committee of a Lodge of Instruction will do well to set themselves rigidly against the practice of allowing refreshment to be consumed in the Lodge Room while the Lodge is open.

The debatable question as to whether smoking should be permitted during the work in a Lodge of Instruction is one which has given rise to widespread discussion, and it is not here intended to argue the *pros* and *cons*. In the recognised Emulation-working Lodges of Instruction smoking is strictly banned; before the official recognition of the Emulation Committee can be obtained, a Lodge of Instruction must incorporate in its By-Laws a clause that both smoking and refreshment in the Lodge Room are prohibited while the Lodge is open for business. In the majority of Lodges of Instruction smoking is allowable; in some, unfortunately, refreshment also. The present writer has been Preceptor in Lodges which permit smoking, as well as those where it is taboo, and he has to confess that he did not find that the enjoyment of tobacco in any way affected the keenness of the work. But where pipes and cigarettes are allowed, the Preceptor will be wise to rule that the *Officers* taking part in the Ceremony should refrain from smoking.

An important question often arising in Lodges of Instruction is as to whether a Brother who is not a subscribing member of a Regular Lodge is eligible for membership. The Board of General Purposes has ruled that Lodges of Instruction are controlled in this connection by Rule 152, *Book of Constitutions*. This rule stipulates that a non-subscribing Brother shall not be permitted to visit any Lodge more than once unless he again becomes a subscribing member of some Lodge, but that the rule does *not* apply to the visits of a Brother to any Lodge of which he has been elected an Honorary Member.* It is obvious, therefore, that a non-subscribing Brother is *not* eligible for membership, but the Lodge of Instruction may surmount the difficulty, if the Brethren so desire, by electing the would-be member to Honorary Membership.

A Lodge of Instruction should always have By-Laws framed as carefully as those of a Regular Lodge, and, if financial considerations will permit, the By-Laws should be printed and circulated among the members. The financial question is often a difficult one in a Lodge of Instruction, but if care is exercised it should be possible to make ends meet with a Joining Fee of, say, 2s. or 2s. 6d. (not an extravagant sum!), a Visiting Fee of 6d., and a weekly Attendance Fee of 6d. Many Lodges of Instruction have an Annual Subscription in place of the weekly Attendance Fee, but, where this is insisted upon, the membership frequently suffers. The wiser plan is to make the Annual Subscription optional, and let those who prefer it pay the weekly Attendance Fee instead.

Lodges of Instruction should meet as frequently as possible if the members are to be kept together and their enthusiasm maintained. Generally speaking, the most successful and popular Lodges of Instruction are those which meet weekly.

* See Chapter XXVI, p. 229.

All the recognised Emulation-working Lodges of Instruction issue a printed syllabus for the session, from which a Brother may see at a glance the Ceremony due for rehearsal on a given date. In many other Lodges of Instruction there is no set programme, and the Brother elected to the chair for an ensuing meeting is at liberty to name the Ceremony he will rehearse. The Emulation practice of a set programme has much to commend it. It is more businesslike, and, the Ceremonies being taken in rotation, a Brother offering himself as Candidate for any particular Ceremony knows that if he progresses through the offices week by week he will reach the Master's chair six weeks later to rehearse the same Ceremony.

In nearly all the recognised Lodges of Instruction Sections from the Lectures * find a regular place in the syllabus. The Masonic Lectures are heard all too seldom; they provide a useful medium for impressing the ritual of the various Degrees on the minds of the Brethren, and afford much valuable instruction and explanation not to be derived from the actual Ceremonies. The Preceptor who hesitates to introduce the Lectures into his curriculum in the belief that he will have difficulty in inducing Brethren to learn them should not be too easily discouraged. An excellent plan is to devote an occasional evening to the working of a Lecture, and to invite the attendance of a team of expert Lecture-

* See Chapters II and III.

workers to deliver the various Sections.* The interest of the Brethren may be awakened by such a demonstration, and Brother Preceptor may be pleasantly surprised to find that in the near future many of his pupils are eager to make their debut as Lecture-workers.

In addition to the Ceremonies and Lectures there are many ways by which a Preceptor may stimulate the interest of his pupils. A Lodge of Instruction, as its name implies, should be a Lodge where Brethren may expect and receive instruction apart from the actual Ritual. Brief addresses by the Preceptor, or some other competent Past Master, on miscellaneous matters of general Masonic interest are always welcome. It is also an excellent practice for the Preceptor to invite queries from the Brethren at all meetings, a plan which will undoubtedly result in many interesting and instructive discussions. Brother Preceptor, however expert he may be, cannot be expected to know everything; no doubt at times he may meet with a query that 'floors' him, but, if his heart is in his task, he can always 'find out' and report at a subsequent meeting.

A final word of advice to Brother Preceptor is that

* The author has organised many such demonstrations of Lecture-working and has afterwards had the pleasure of learning that they had beneficial effect. He will be pleased at any time to arrange such a demonstration at a Lodge of Instruction if communicated with through the publisher of this Manual.

he should make his teaching as *individual* as possible. The Preceptor who endeavours to take a *personal interest* in the efforts of his pupils will earn not only their confidence and respect, but their friendship and affection. It is by such methods that the Preceptor will make his Lodge of Instruction what every such Lodge should be, a weekly assembly of a happy band of Brothers, all imbued with the one aim to fit themselves to discharge their duties in their respective Lodges with that dignity, decorum, and accuracy which should be the distinguishing mark of all Masonic Ceremonial.

CHAPTER XXIX

SMOKING AT REFRESHMENT *

AT what precise point during the post-prandial
period may permission be granted for the Brethren
to smoke, in conformity with the generally accepted
rules of Masonic etiquette and courtesy? It is a
safe prophecy that in the majority of cases such
permission is anxiously awaited by a large per-
centage of Brethren eager for the solace and enjoyment of the fragrant weed which William Lilye, the
famous fifteenth-century grammarian, styled 'our
holy herb nicotian.'

The exact point at which permission may be
given for Brethren to 'light up' did not enter the
range of controversy until very recent years. That
it has now become a subject of controversy there
can be little doubt; varying opinions are advanced,
each one claiming to be authoritative, and acri-
monious disputes have arisen among the several
champions of ceremonial etiquette who find themselves at variance. Some there are who declare that

* Most of the material in this chapter was included in an
article by the author entitled " Brethren, You May Smoke,"
published in *The Freemason* on 3rd November 1928, and now
reproduced here by the courtesy of the editor of that journal.

smoking is permissible as soon as the toast of 'The Grand Master' has been honoured; others that it should be deferred until after the toast of 'The Grand Lodge Officers' has been submitted; still others who stoutly aver that adherents to My Lady Nicotine must hold their desires in check until the last-mentioned toast has been responded to. A few sticklers go even further and withhold the eagerly awaited permission until the toast of 'The Provincial Grand Master' has been received. This extreme, however, applies only in the case of a few Provinces and scarcely comes within the scope of a chapter dealing with generalities.

If disputing Brethren base their respective opinions on the observance of correct 'etiquette,' it is interesting to examine the word itself. The word is French, and the old French *estiquette* or *estiquet* meant a 'label' or 'ticket.' Randle Cotgrave, the Cheshire lexicographer, whose French-English dictionary, published in the second decade of the seventeenth century, is still a work of valuable historical importance, explained the word in French as a 'billet' for the benefit or advantage of him that receives it; a form of introduction. Also, as a notice fixed at the gate of a court of law. The development of meaning in French from a 'label' to 'ceremonial rules' is not difficult to follow. For our purpose the generally accepted definition of the word in its broad sense may be taken to mean 'the correct social observances required by good breeding.'

Obviously 'good breeding' and 'social observances' may be assumed to embrace loyalty to the
Throne and due and becoming respect to the
reigning monarch. Hence an assembly of gentlemen dining ceremoniously—whether they be
members of our Fraternity or not—refrain from
smoking until after the toast of 'The King,' on any
occasion when it is customary to honour the loyal
toast. Loyalty and proper submission to the
Throne have dictated the custom. It would be
superfluous to emphasise that members of the Craft
yield first place to no section of society in the
matter of loyalty to the Sovereign. Here, then, we
have the indisputable, basic fact, upon which all
Brethren will be in agreement, that cigars and
cigarettes must remain unlighted until after the
loyal toast.

As the King is the supreme ruler of all who owe
allegiance to the flags of Britain, her Dominions
and Dependencies, so the M.W. the Grand Master
is the supreme ruler of all Brethren attached to
Lodges under the English Constitution. Here
again we have sure guidance; loyalty and respectful
submission to the Grand Master indicate that,
among Freemasons, smoking is taboo until the
second toast on the list has been received with
customary honours.

Of recent years the question has been complicated
by the new-fangled assertion that the cigarette
which many like to enjoy with a sorbet is 'out of

order' unless the toast of 'The King' has first been honoured. Whence came this somewhat dogmatic interference with long-established custom? What vestige of authority have the voluntary champions of etiquette for their dogmatism? For many years the cigarette served with the sorbet has been an accepted custom, and not until the past three or four years has a hint ever been heard that the harmless custom outraged decency or loyalty.

There is little doubt that a general consensus of opinion would be to the effect that smoking is permissible directly after the Grand Master's toast has been honoured. As already mentioned, there are a few scrupulous sticklers in some Provinces who would strain the loyalty and patience of the Brethren by withholding permission until after the toast of 'The Provincial Grand Master,' but such extremes are few and far between. A Province is entitled to establish its own customs, however arbitrary they may appear at first sight. One can only sympathise with the Brethren compelled to submit to such capricious dicta.

The whims of faddists are notoriously infectious. Let the self-appointed advocates of any artificial reform shout loudly enough, and some will be found to accept them at their own valuation. Hence has sprung up in many directions the incongruous custom of giving the loyal toast in the middle of the banquet. In all spheres of life one is sometimes surprised to note how many are to be found willing to follow blindly the lead of self-constituted pioneers of so-called reform. It is still more surprising to find that in the Masonic '*Calendar*' of one of the most influential Provinces it is definitely laid down that:

"If, in the middle of dinner, the Brethren want to smoke with the sorbet, the Master should then give the toast of The King to allow them to do so."

To all save the slavish purist the mid-prandial cigarette is an accepted accompaniment of the sorbet, one which may be enjoyed *with* that dainty, not to be lighted *before* the sorbet is served, nor retained *after* it is finished. It is not intended nor regarded as a smoke *per se*; therefore its transient intrusion is not generally viewed as an infringement of the ruling already stated, viz. that an assembly of gentlemen, dining ceremoniously, refrain from smoking until after the loyal toast.

The incongruity of the direction quoted from a Provincial '*Calendar*' is apparent at a glance. The proposing of the loyal toast by the Master in the middle of dinner conveys tacit permission to the Brethren that they may smoke freely and without restraint, irrespective of the sorbet or any other accompaniment, quite heedless of the universally accepted restriction that smoking may *not* be indulged in at any Masonic gathering until after the toast of 'The M.W. Grand Master.' If it is a contravention of the canons of etiquette to indulge

18

in a few whiffs with the sorbet before the loyal toast, it is equally a violation of those canons to do so prior to the toast of the Grand Master. However arbitrary a command may be, one may accept it with good grace if it has the merit of consistency; there is nothing consistent in the example quoted.

The regrettable consequence of this new-born custom of giving the loyal toast in the middle of dinner is to be seen in many directions. Brethren whose appetites are already assuaged continue smoking during the remainder of the meal, and their flagrant defiance of all accepted rules of courtesy often passes unchecked by those self-same 'guardians of etiquette' who throw up their hands in punctilious horror at the sight of a spiral of tobacco-smoke during the consumption of the sorbet unless the loyal toast has first been submitted.

The great body of the Craft is admittedly loyal to the expressed wishes of its rulers. Uncertainty and confusion would be banished by a direct hint from the usual recognised quarter from which all Masonic authority emanates. In the absence of any such hint, common sense and ordinary courtesy would seem to dictate that the toast of 'The King' is entirely out of place until after Grace has been offered.

CHAPTER XXX

MASONIC DON'TS

DON'T, if you are the Master of a Lodge, wear your Master's Collar and Jewel when visiting. Such a practice is contrary to the *Constitutions*.

DON'T be slovenly with your Sns. Remember that all Sq....s, L....s, and P.rp....c...rs are true and proper Sns. to know a Mason by. Remember, too, that all Masonic Sns. should be given *silently*.

DON'T make any preliminary 'pointing' motion when giving the P.Sn. of an E.A. The r.h. should be brought *direct to position* with the th.ex.i.t.f.o.a. Sq.t.t.l.o.t.w.-p.

DON'T forget the difference between the Sn. of R. and the Sn. of F. In the latter the th. is sq....d and the Sn. is *drawn*. In the former the th. is *not* sq....d and the Sn. is *dropped*.

DON'T forget that when discharging the P.Sn. in any Degree the h. should be kept *open*.

DON'T omit to 'recover' the P.Sn. of the Third

Degree. There is *only one exception* to this rule. (See para. 11, p. 236.)

DON'T forget the Sp. before *any* Sn., with the *single exception* of the Sn. of R. Actually this is *not* a Masonic Sn. It would be more accurately described as the *attitude* of R.

DON'T propose a Candidate for Initiation unless you feel *absolutely certain* that he is the right man, not only for Freemasonry, but also for membership of your particular Lodge. You will be wise to make it a rigid rule *never* to propose a Candidate unless he is an intimate friend whose character you know thoroughly.

DON'T, when you are Master, permit any adjournment to another room during the Installation Ceremony for the purpose of permitting the members of the Board of I.M.'s to partake of refreshment. As recently as March 1926 the practice has been definitely condemned by the Board of General Purposes as irregular and a contravention of the undertaking given to the Home Secretary in 1902 by the Grand Registrar that the Masonic authorities would condemn the practice of consuming any intoxicating liquors in Lodge, *or on premises directly associated with the Lodge*, in connection with the Ceremony of Installation. It is to be regretted that some otherwise well-conducted Lodges continue flagrantly to violate this ruling.

DON'T permit your Lodge Committee to be styled your 'Board of General Purposes' if you have influence to prevent it. The *Book of Constitutions* limits the use of the title 'Board' to certain bodies specified therein. 'Standing *Committee*' or 'Lodge *Committee*' are the descriptions which should be employed by advisory bodies in private Lodges.

DON'T frame your Grand Lodge Certificate and publicly exhibit it on your business premises, even in your private office. Such a practice can only be interpreted as an endeavour to turn Freemasonry to commercial advantage, and is emphatically deprecated by the Masonic authorities.

DON'T talk to your immediate neighbours during the progress of a Ceremony in Lodge. The slightest whisper sometimes carries much further than the whisperer realises. Remember that the Master is concentrating on his task, and he may be nervy; the slightest interruption may throw him right out of his stride.

DON'T ever laugh, or even smile, if there is an amusing hitch in the work during a Ceremony. We do hear and see some amusing happenings at times, but any hint of mirth may utterly destroy those solemn impressions which *should* be created in the Candidate's mind.

DON'T loll and sprawl in your seat in Lodge even

if you happen to be feeling weary and, perchance, somewhat bored. You may have heard it all a hundred times, but it is the Candidate's first time; his interest will undoubtedly be stimulated if the Brethren are interested.

DON'T be in too much of a hurry to join a number of Lodges, or to enter the 'Side' Degrees. Pause to consider the financial aspect. Remember that Masonic expenditure should always be 'without detriment,' etc.

DON'T hesitate to enter the Order of the Holy Royal Arch. This is *not* a 'Side' Degree, it is a part of 'pure Antient Masonry.' (See Rule 1, *B. of C.*)

DON'T speak of Officers of London Rank as 'London Rankers.' It is discourteous and offensive.

DON'T, if you are an Officer of London Rank or of Provincial or District Grand Rank, attend an Installation Meeting in Undress Regalia.

DON'T make the work of the Treasurer or Secretary harder by neglecting to reply promptly to their communications.

DON'T forget that the Tyler is a 'Brother.' A handshake and a cheery word of greeting may mean much to him.

DON'T presume upon your Masonic association with those in a higher social station than yourself.

Don't be stand-offish in your Masonic association with those in a *lower* social station than your own. We meet on the square, and part on the level.

Don't wear Masonic charms on your watch-chain, or as any other form of personal adornment. It simply 'isn't done.'

Don't indulge in noisy behaviour at the banquet. You would not shout across the room at a private dinner-party. Why do it at a Masonic dinner?

Don't talk or move about the dining-room while an artiste is on the platform. The musical entertainment may at times be of rather in-different quality, and many of us may wish that it could be dispensed with; but, when such an entertainment is provided, common courtesy demands that the artistes should be granted silence and the undivided attention of their audience.

Don't address the Master as 'Worshipful *Sir*' either at Labour or Refreshment; it should *always* be 'Worshipful *Master*.' And Don't ever be guilty of addressing the Master as 'W.M.' Abbreviations such as 'W.M.,' 'S.W.,' etc., are permissible in printing, but no Officer should ever be addressed orally by an abbreviated title.

Don't ever tell (or encourage) questionable anec-dotes in a Masonic atmosphere.

Don't forget that 'Evening Dress' means *Masonic* Evening Dress and that *white* waistcoats should *not* be worn. With full Evening Dress a white tie is correct. A black tie should always be worn with a Dinner Jacket.

[Under date 12th June 1933, the M.W. Grand Master, in response to a suggestion submitted to him by the M.W. Pro G.M., granted authority for white waistcoats to be worn with Evening Dress at Masonic assemblies, at the discretion of Provincial and District Grand Masters and Masters of Lodges. A black waistcoat is, therefore, no longer obligatory.]

Don't forget that 'Morning Dress' *means* Morning Dress, *not* a light Lounge Suit. Brethren who should know better sometimes err in this connection.

Don't become a 'knife and fork' Mason; you had better drop out altogether.

Don't criticise the Preceptor at your Lodge of Instruction even though you may consider him too autocratic, or perhaps incompetent. Remember that he is doing his best and that he is giving his time to try and assist his Brethren.

Don't, if you are an expert ritualist, be too ready to condemn the Brother who is not. Remember that we cannot *all* be 'stars.'

DON'T condemn any practice as *wrong* because it happens to be contrary to the custom of your own Lodge, or because it differs from that which you have been taught in your Lodge of Instruction. Remember that *your* custom *may* be the wrong one.

DON'T imagine that word-perfection of Ritual is the Alpha and Omega of Freemasonry. It is important, but there are other things far more important.

DON'T think that you have done something extraordinarily clever if you win the silver matchbox at the Emulation Lodge of Improvement. It simply means that you have a good memory—and that you have had some *luck*.

DON'T forget the first of the Three Grand Principles upon which our Order is founded. Keep that Principle ever in mind and 'Profit and Pleasure' will be the result.

LODGES OF INSTRUCTION RECOGNISED BY THE COMMITTEE OF THE EMULATION
LODGE OF IMPROVEMENT.

LONDON.

Name of Lodge.	Place of Meeting.	Day of Meeting.	Hour.
			P.M.
Langton	Simpson's, Poultry, E.C. .	THURSDAY. October to April inclusive . . .	5.30
Kirby	Midland Grand Hotel, St Pancras . .	TUESDAY. Throughout the year	7
London Rifle Brigade .	Pimms' Imperial Restaurant, 57 Old Bailey, E.C.4.	WEDNESDAY. October to April inclusive . .	6.15
St Bride . . .	Pimms' Restaurant, 94–96 Bishopsgate, E.C.	WEDNESDAY. October to May inclusive . - .	5.45
Peter Gilkes . . .	Horn's Hotel, Kennington Park, S.E.11 .	THURSDAY. Throughout the year . . .	7.30
Chisel	Great Eastern Hotel, Liverpool Street, E.C.	MONDAY. Sept. to May inclusive . . .	5.30
Strong Man and Cornish .	Queen's Head Hotel, Theobalds Road, W.C.1	TUESDAY. Third Tuesday in Sept. to second in June	6.30
Hiram	Mark Masons' Hall, Great Queen Street, W.C.2.	Alternate MONDAYS. October to May . . .	6.30
Polytechnic . . .	309 Regent Street, W.1. . . .	THURSDAY. October to March inclusive . .	7
Telephone . . .	Mansion House Station Restaurant, E.C.4 .	TUESDAY. Sept. to April inclusive . . .	6
Royal Athelstan . .	White Horse Restaurant, 100 High Holborn, W.C.1.	MONDAY. October to April inclusive . .	6.15
Horus	The "Mitre," Chancery Lane, E.C. . .	TUESDAY. Third Tuesday in Sept. to last in April .	6.30
Hardware . . .	White Horse Restaurant, 100 High Holborn, W.C.1.	WEDNESDAY. Third in Sept. to third in April inclusive	6.30
Ad Astra . . .	Bedford Head Hotel, Maiden Lane, Strand, W.C.2.	WEDNESDAY. October to April inclusive . .	6
Campbell . . .	Princes Head Hotel, Princes Street, Westminster.	THURSDAY. Third Thursday in Sept. to last in April	6.15
Papyrus . . .	Mansion House Station Restaurant, E.C.4 .	WEDNESDAY. October to April inclusive . .	6
City Liveries . . .	Painters' Hall, Little Trinity Lane, E.C.4 .	TUESDAY. October to April inclusive . .	5.30
Preceptors' . . .	White Horse Restaurant, 100 High Holborn, W.C.1.	WEDNESDAY. May to August inclusive . .	6.30
Amici	"The Bedford," Southampton Buildings, Holborn, E.C.1.	MONDAY. September to April inclusive . .	6.45

PROVINCES.

St James . . .	Masonic Hall, Wretham Road, Handsworth	MONDAY. Second and fourth, Sept. to May .	6.30
West Lancashire . .	Angel Hotel, Dale Street, Liverpool . .	WEDNESDAY. Sept. to March inclusive . .	7
St Albans . . .	Town Hall, St Albans . . .	WEDNESDAY. Second and fourth, October to May	8
Fenwick . . .	Masonic Hall, Park Terrace, Sunderland .	First WEDNESDAY. October to May inclusive .	7
Berries . . .	Masonic Hall, Maidenhead . . .	TUESDAY. Second and fourth, Sept. to April .	7.30
Napier-Clavering .	Masonic Hall, 232 Shields Road, Newcastle-on-Tyne.	MONDAY. Third and fourth, October to April	7
Letchworth . .	Town Hall, Stretford . . .	THURSDAY. Second and fourth, Sept. to April	7.15
Honour . . .	Masonic Temple, Wolverhampton .	MONDAY. Second and fourth, October to May	6.30
Josiah Wedgwood .	Freemasons' Hall, Cheapside, Hanley .	MONDAY. Preceding fourth Thursday, Sept. to April	7.30
Jordan . . .	Masonic Hall, Torquay . . .	Last MONDAY. Throughout the year . .	7.30
Noel Money . .	Ship Hotel, Weybridge . . .	MONDAY. Last in Sept. to third in March .	8.15
Shipcote . . .	Masonic Hall, Gateshead . . .	MONDAY. Second Monday, Sept. to June .	7.30
Southport . . .	Masonic Hall, Southport . . .	Fortnightly. Different days . . .	8
Earl of Clarendon .	Halsey Masonic Hall, Watford . .	MONDAY. October to April . . .	8
General . . .	Chamber of Commerce Buildings, New Street, Birmingham.	FRIDAY. Sept. to May	6.30
George Rankin .	162 Lower Addiscombe Road, Croydon	WEDNESDAY. Throughout the year . .	8
Canute . . .	Mordaunt Hall, Mordaunt Road, Southampton.	TUESDAY. October to May . . .	7
Royal Victorian Jubilee	King's Head Hotel, Romford . .	MONDAY. October to May inclusive . .	7.30
Cheshire Emulation .	St John's C. of E. School, Altrincham .	First FRIDAY and third TUESDAY. Sept. to April	7.30
St Modwens . .	Masonic Hall, Burton-on-Trent . .	Second and fourth THURSDAY. September to May .	6.30
East Croydon . .	162 Lower Addiscombe Road, Croydon	TUESDAY. Throughout the year . . .	8
Hundred of Wirral .	The Crypt, St Paul's Church, Argyle Street, Birkenhead.	MONDAY. September to March . . .	7.30
Malden . . .	"Royal Oak," Coombe Road, New Malden	MONDAY. October to April . . .	8
Shirley Park . .	Café Royal, Croydon . . .	MONDAY. October to May . . .	8
Heath Park . .	"Durham Arms," Brentwood Road, Romford	TUESDAY. October to May . . .	7.30

APPENDIX B.

TABLE OF K...KS.

(NOTE.—" K "=1 K...k. ' 1,' ' 2,' ' 3 '=K...ks of First, Second, and Third Degrees.)

	First Degree.					Second Degree.					Third Degree.				
	W.M.	S.W.	J.W.	I.G.	T.	W.M.	S.W.	J.W.	I.G.	T.	W.M.	S.W.	J.W.	I.G.	T.
OPENINGS.															
Beginning	K	K	K	o	o	K	K	K	o	o	K	K	K	o	o
Seeing Lodge Properly T...d	o	o	o	1	1	o	o	o	1	1	o	o	o	2	2
Reporting Lodge Properly T...d	o	o	1	o	o	o	o	1	o	o	o	o	2	o	o
Ending	1	1	1	1	1	2*	2*	2*	2*	2	3*	3*	3*	3*	3

(Muffled when Candidate is outside.)

	First Degree.					Second Degree.					Third Degree.				
CLOSINGS.															
Beginning	K	K	K	o	o	K	K	K	o	o	K	K	K	o	o
Proving Lodge Close T...d	o	o	o	1	1	o	o	o	2	2	o	o	o	3	3
Reporting Lodge Close T...d	o	o	1	o	o	o	o	2	o	o	o	o	3	o	o
Ending	1	1	1	1	1	2	2	2	2	2	3	3	3	3	3
CEREMONIES.															
Reporting Candidate at door	o	o	o	o	1	o	o	o	o	1	o	o	o	o	2
" " " "	o	o	1	o	o	o	o	o	o	o	o	o	o	o	o
Before Pr...r	K	K	K	o	o	K	K	K	o	o	K	K	K	o	o
Before ' Brn. will take notice '	K	K	K	o	o	K	K	K	o	o	K	K	K	o	o
Before Ob.	K	K	K	o	o	K	K	K	o	o	K	K	K	o	o
Restoration of L...t	K	o	o	o	o	..	..	..	..	..	..	..	..	..	..
† 2nd T.B., when W.M. refers to letter G	..	..	..	..	..	K	K	K	o	o	..	..	..	..	..

RESUMING.—K...ks of the Degree into which the Lodge is resumed.

	First Degree.					Second Degree.					Third Degree.				
‡ CALLING OFF AND ON.															
Beginning	K	K	K	o	o	K	K	K	o	o	K	K	K	o	o
Ending	K	K	K	o	o	K	K	K	o	o	K	K	K	o	o

To SUMMON THE TYLER.—Two quick, loud K...ks at any stage.

* At Emulation Lodge of Improvement when the Lodge is Opened or Resumed in the Second or Third Degree, and a Candidate is in the anteroom awaiting admission to the higher Degree, the W.M. and W.'s give muffled K.'s. In such cases the I.G. does not communicate the K.'s to the Tyler ; he stands in his place and gives the K.'s on his cuff. The reason for these muffled K.'s is so that the Can. shall not hear the K.'s of a Degree to which he has not yet been admitted. A few regular Emulation-working Lodges adopt a similar practice, but the general custom is for all K.'s to be given aloud. The practice followed at Emulation Lodge of Improvement has the disadvantage that the Tyler is likely to be left in a state of uncertainty as to the exact point at which the Lodge is Opened or Resumed in the higher Degree.

† If the Master is giving the Lecture the K. at the W.M.'s pedestal is given by the I.P.M.

‡ Here the K...ks go round in reverse order—(1) J.W., (2) S.W., (3) W.M.

APPENDIX C

LETTER FROM V.W. BRO. SIR EDWARD LETCH-
WORTH, GRAND SECRETARY 1892 TO 1917.

UNITED GRAND LODGE OF ENGLAND,
FREEMASONS' HALL,
GREAT QUEEN STREET, LONDON, W.C.,
November 22, 1912.

DEAR SIR AND BROTHER,—

I am in receipt of your letter of the 20th inst.,
and am pleased to learn that a correct rendering of
the Ritual is a subject of concern to the members
of your Lodge.

While it is true that no *edict* has ever been issued
by Grand Lodge as to any particular working being
accepted, nor is it considered compulsory that
Lodges should conform to what is termed the
"Emulation" system of ritual, on the other hand
it is an historical fact that Grand Lodge in 1816
definitely adopted and gave its approval to the
system of working submitted to it by the Lodge
of Reconciliation, and it is also a fact that this is the
system which the Emulation Lodge of Improvement was founded in 1823 to teach, and which is
taught by that Lodge to-day.

The late Bro. Thomas Fenn, who was considered
the most able exponent of Masonic Ritual of his

day, always held the opinion that the "Emulation" working was authorised, and that opinion is also held by Bro. Sudlow, his successor in the teaching of that system.   Certainly no other system of ritual has received at any time the official approval of Grand Lodge.—I am,

Yours fraternally,

E. LETCHWORTH, G.S.

W. BRO. W. P. CAMPBELL-EVERDEN, L.R.,
    Lodge No. 19, London.

INDEX

ABBREVIATED titles, 279.
Absence of Master, 204, 205, 212.
Absence of Officers, 94, 161, 233.
Accuracy of record, 179, 180, 219.
Addresses, Ceremonial, 167, 168.
Addresses, Installation, 246.
Adjourn, Lodge cannot, 198, 199.
Admission, demanding, 99, 100.
Admission of Candidates, 100, 101, 102, 106, 107, 108, 109, 132, 136, 138, 140, 145, 149, 150, 153, 154.
Admission of Grand Officers after Opening, 165.
Admission of visitors, 165.
Admission, refusing, 221.
Advance as a F.C., 145.
Advance as a Mason, 150.
Advancement by rotation, 14, 111, 112.
'Advancing' by Candidates, 145.
 from First to Second Degree, 107, 108, 137, 138, 139, 150, 151, 152, 153, 200, 201, 208, 209, 243.

'Advancing' from Second to Third Degree, 108, 109, 139, 140, 141, 144, 145, 146, 147, 148, 149, 150, 201, 202, 209, 210, 244.
 from West to East, Second Degree, 151.
 from West to East, Third Degree, 147.
 to ped., First Degree, 133.
'Alarms' or 'Reports,' 90.
'All charged,' 196.
'All poor and distressed Masons,' 87.
Almoner, 117, 118, 119, 120, 155.
 Jewel of, 117.
Alms-dish, 135.
Ampthill, Lord, 35.
Ancient Charges and Regulations, 176, 245.
'Ancients,' Grand Lodge of, 25, 29.
Anderson, Dr James, 55.
Anecdotes, questionable, 251, 279.
Angle of the Square, 139.
Announcement of Candidates, 100, 106, 107, 108, 109, 199, 200, 201, 202.
'Answer,' 133.
Anteroom, 91, 131, 161.
Anthem, National, 250.
Antient Charges, 14.

Antient Landmarks, 192.
Antiquity, Lodge of, 56.
Appeal to higher authority, 220.
Appendices, 283, 284, 285, 286, 287, 288.
Applause, Masonic, 168.
Appointment of Officers, 111, 112.
Apron, when worn under the coat, 161.
Arch, Holy Royal, 278.
Articles of Union, 26, 41.
Artistes, courtesy to, 279.
Artistes, professional, 250, 279.
'Assemblage of Brethren,' 15.
Assistant Director of Ceremonies, 117, 120, 121, 122, 163, 172, 173.
  position in Lodge, 163.
  should be a P.M., 121.
Assistant Provincial Grand Master, visit by, 246.
Assistant Secretary, 111, 112, 113, 118, 120.
  Jewel of, 111.
Attendance at Grand Lodge, 193, 194, 231.
Attendance Book, 92, 161, 178, 230.
Attitude of Reverence, 276.
Authorised Ritual, 24, 25, 35, 287, 288.

BAD character, 221.
Badge of a F.C., 152, 208.
Badge of a Mason, 135, 205, 207.
Badge of a Master Mason, 149, 210.
Badge of every Mason, 205.
Badge of Innocence, 205.
Badge must be removed, 209, 210.

Badham, R. L., 62.
Ballots, 128, 228, 229, 247, 248.
Ballots, announcement of, 229.
Ballots, collective, 229, 247.
Ballots, Deacons attending to, 127.
Ballots, not necessary for Honorary Members, 229.
Banquet, 173, 174, 195, 215, 216, 279.
Behaviour, 195, 216, 250, 277, 278, 279.
Black, J. J., 32, 68, 69.
Black ties, 280.
Board of Benevolence, 212.
Boards. See Tracing Boards.
Boards, Social, 195.
Book of Constitutions, 85, 93, 111, 114, 120, 155, 157, 164, 179, 181, 187, 192, 204, 211, 212, 213, 218, 220, 221, 222, 223, 224, 226, 228, 229, 230, 232, 245, 247, 255, 256, 260, 264, 277, 278.
Bowing to the W.M., 106, 107.
'Bright Morning Star,' 149.
Bristol-working, 24.
British Lodge, 29.
Broadfoot, Philip, 57.
Burlington Lodge, 96.
By-Laws, to be supplied to Candidates, 228, 247.

CABLE-TOW, 134.
Caduceus, 142.
Calling Off and On, 198, 203, 204, 239, 240, 241, 248.
Calling the Lodge from Labour to Refreshment, 204, 239, 240, 241, 248.

Calvert, A. F., 40, 41, 46, 50.
Campbell-Everden, W. P., 288.
Candidate(s), admission of, 100, 101, 102, 106, 107, 108, 109, 132, 136, 138, 140, 145, 149, 150, 153, 154.
advancement, 133, 140, 145, 147, 150, 151, 152, 154.
announcing of, 100, 106, 107, 108, 109, 199, 200, 201, 202.
awaiting admission, 99, 285, 286.
balloting for, 228, 229.
best method of controlling, 132.
care necessary in proposing, 276.
directions to, 126.
entrusting, 134, 137, 144, 150, 152, 200, 201, 208, 242, 243.
examinations, 135, 137, 144, 147, 150, 151, 152, 200, 201, 202, 206, 207, 208, 209.
first impressions, 130, 131.
for Initiation, 90, 91.
for Passing, 90.
for Raising, 90.
Initiation of, 106, 107, 132, 133, 134, 135, 136, 137, 153, 154, 199, 200, 206, 207, 242, 243.
Investitures, 135, 149, 152, 207, 208, 210.
nervous, 131.
Passing of, 107, 108, 137, 138, 139, 150, 151, 152, 153, 200, 201, 208, 209, 243.
position for Charge, 136, 137.

Candidate(s), position for second T.B., 139, 153.
position for Traditional History, 149.
presence of a, 90.
presentation of, 206, 207, 208, 209, 210.
proposition of, 230, 276.
Raising of, 108, 109, 139, 140, 141, 144, 145, 146, 147, 148, 149, 150, 201, 202, 209, 210, 244.
reporting of, 106, 107, 108, 199, 200, 201, 202.
should always be allowed to leave the Lodge to restore himself, 136, 148, 153.
should receive By-Laws, 228, 247.
when reported as 'Mr,' 100, 206.
when under Master's control, 134, 152.
Casting vote, 220.
Ceremonial address, 167, 168.
Ceremonies. See under 'Initiation,' 'Installation,' 'Passing,' and 'Raising.'
Certificates not to be publicly exhibited, 277.
Chalkley, S., 32, 33, 51.
'Challenging,' 195, 250.
Chaplain, 155, 184, 187, 188, 189, 190, 214, 234.
Jewel of, 187, 188.
position of, 188.
Charge after Initiation, 136, 137, 189, 243.
Charge, interruption of, by gavel, 79.
Charity Box, 117, 118.
Charms, Masonic, 279.
Cheques, 185.

Churchill, Lord St John Spencer, 47.
Clare, Martin, 55.
Closing Ode, 115, 237.
Closing the Lodge generally, 105, 214, 237.
  in the Second Degree, 105, 237.
  in the Third Degree, 104, 105, 236, 237.
Clothing, Masonic, 161, 173.
Collective ballots, 229, 247.
Compasses, 95, 101, 102, 109, 161, 214, 235, 242.
Compasses, method for I.G. to apply, 101.
Compasses should point towards W.M., 214, 235.
Complete Record - holders, List of, 63, 64.
Confirmation of Minutes, 179, 218, 219, 247.
Cooper, 30, 31.
Corinthian Order, 198.
Cornucopia, 95.
Criticism of Emulation, 73, 75, 76.
Crossed Swords, 96.
Crucefix, Dr R. T., 44, 51.
Cuff, knocks on, 285, 286.

DATES of Meetings, 198.
Dawson, W. A., 32.
Deacons, 94, 101, 106, 108, 109, 123, 124, 125, 126, 127, 128, 129, 165.
  Jewels of, 123, 142, 143.
  make or mar the Ceremonies, 124.
  must know the Ritual, 125.
  See also under 'Junior Deacon' and 'Senior Deacon.'

Death of Master, 204, 212.
Declaring Offices vacant, 171, 245.
'Demanding' admission, 99, 100.
Demeanour in Lodge, 277, 278.
'Deputy' *v.* 'Assistant,' 120.
Deputy District Grand Master, visit by, 246.
Deputy Grand Master, visit by, 246.
Deputy Provincial Grand Master, visit by, 246.
Desaguliers, Dr John, 55.
'Differences' in the Lodge, 189, 190.
Differences of working, 76, 77, 78, 79, 80, 81.
'Dine in Collars,' 173.
Dinner jackets, 161, 280.
Director(s) of Ceremonies, 74, 88, 89, 94, 95, 119, 120, 121, 122, 155, 156, 157, 158, 159, 160, 161, 162, 163, 164, 165, 166, 167, 168, 169, 170, 171, 172, 173, 174, 175, 192, 196, 233.
  absence of, at Emulation, 155, 170.
  absence of, in private Lodges, 156, 157.
  criticism of, 155.
  duties at Refreshment, 173, 174.
  general hints for, 161, 162, 163, 164, 165, 166, 167, 168, 169, 170, 171, 172, 173, 174.
  must be a P.M., 159.
  position in Lodge, 163.
  qualifications of, 158, 159.
Dispensations, 173, 247.
Displacing an Officer, 224.

Disputes, 189, 190.

Distressed Brethren, 117.

District Grand Master, visit by, 246.

District Grand Rank, 163, 165, 167, 173, 215, 278.

' Don'ts,' Masonic, 275, 276, 277, 278, 279, 280, 281.

Door of the Lodge, 97, 98.
  position of the, 98.

Doric Order, 204.

Dove and Olive Branch, 123, 142.

Dowley, John, 30, 31, 32.

' Drawn ' v. ' Dropped,' 245, 275.

Drawn sword, 101.

Dress, 161, 280.

Dress, evening, 161, 280.

Dress, morning, 161, 280.

' Dropped ' v. ' Drawn,' 245, 275.

Dunckerley, Thomas, 55.

E.A., P.Sn. of, 275.

Elected Officers, 88, 184.

Election of Master, 218, 248.

Election of Master and Treasurer, 248.

Emblem of Plenty, 95.

Emblem of Restraint, 95.

Emergency Meetings, 179, 198, 247.

Employer's Liability, 182.

Emulation, differences from, 76, 77, 78, 79, 80, 81.

Emulation, What is ?, 23, 24, 25, 26, 27, 28, 29, 30, 31, 32, 33, 34, 35, 36.

Emulation and the Grand Stewards, 37, 38, 39, 40, 41, 42, 43, 44, 45, 46, 47, 48, 49, 50, 51, 52.

Emulation Committee, 17, 31, 32, 33, 34, 35, 39, 46, 65, 66, 67, 68, 69, 70, 71, 72.

Emulation Lectures, 53, 54, 55, 56, 57, 58, 59.

Emulation Lodge of Improvement, 17, 18, 23, 24, 25, 26, 27, 28, 29, 30, 31, 32, 33, 34, 35, 36, 37, 38, 39, 43, 44, 45, 46, 49, 51, 52, 56, 57, 58, 59, 60, 61, 62, 65, 66, 67, 68, 69, 70, 71, 72, 73, 97, 128, 137, 140, 144, 155, 157, 158, 168, 169, 170, 172, 234, 281, 283, 284, 285, 286, 287.

control of, 17, 31, 33, 65.

date of founding, 24.

history of, 24, 25, 26, 27, 28, 29, 30, 31, 32, 33, 34.

Emulation match-box, 60, 61, 62, 63, 64, 281.

Emulation Minutes destroyed, 65.

Emulation Secretaries, 34.

Emulation system, 17, 24, 25, 31, 90, 125, 171, 172, 176, 287.

Emulation Treasurers, 33, 34.

Emulation-working, criticism of, 73, 75, 76.

Entertainment, silence during, 279.

Etiquette as to smoking, 248, 249, 269, 270, 271, 272, 273, 274.

Euclid, 47th Proposition of, 211.

Evening dress, 161, 280.

Exclusion, permanent, 222, 223.

Exclusion, temporary, 221, 222.

Exclusion and Expulsion, 223.

Exhortation, Third Degree, 141, 148.
Expenditure, Masonic, 278.
Expert Ritualists, 280.
Expulsion, 223.

F.F.F., 214.
F.Ps. of F., 244.
Fenn, Thomas, 32, 33, 34, 51, 287.
First Great Light, 235.
First impressions, 130, 131.
Foreign Constitutions, Visitors from, 166.
' Fourth Degree,' 194.
Franck, J. E., 34.

G. or R. Sn., 166, 236.
G. or T., communication of, 135.
Gavelling, heavy, 195.
Gilkes, Peter, 28, 29, 30, 31, 32, 33, 39, 42, 57, 59.
Gloves, white, 161.
Grand Director(s) of Ceremonies, 156, 157, 169, 174.
Grand Lodge Minutes, 25, 88.
Grand Master, visit by, 246.
    receiving communications from, 238.
Grand Officers, entering after Lodge is open, 165.
    precedence of, 164, 166, 167, 168.
    rights of, 99, 249, 250.
    salutes to, 166, 167.
    seating at Refreshment, 173, 174.
    seating in Lodge, 164, 165.
    titles of, 167, 168.
Grand Stewards and Emulation, 37, 38, 39, 40, 41, 42, 43, 44, 45, 46, 47, 48, 49, 50, 51, 52.

Grand Stewards' Lodge, 37, 38, 39, 40, 41, 42, 43, 44, 45, 46, 47, 48, 49, 50, 51, 52, 55, 56, 59.
' Greetings ' v. ' Salutes,' 168, 169.
Grenfell, J. S. Granville, 51, 156, 169, 174.
Grey, Robert, 51.

HALT, Candidate must, when giving Sns., 146.
' Halt while I report,' 106, 107, 109.
Hand to be kept open, 275.
Harmony, disturbing, 14.
Harper, Edwards, 28, 41, 42, 43, 51.
Health, Symbol of, 142.
' Hearty Good Wishes,' 239.
' Hele,' pronunciation of, 242.
Hemming, Samuel, 41, 51, 55, 56.
Hermes, 142.
Hervey, John, 33.
Hextall, W. B., 30.
Hiram Abiff, 198.
Hiram, King of Tyre, 204.
Hockley, F., 51.
Holy Royal Arch, 278.
Honorary Members, 229, 230, 265.
    status of, 229, 230, 265.
' Honorary ' Secretary, 182.
Hutchinson, William, 55.

IGNORANCE, 73, 212, 221.
Immediate Past Master, 102, 128, 169, 170, 172, 188, 201, 209, 211, 212, 213, 214, 215, 216, 234, 235, 285, 286.

Immediate Past Master, duties at Refreshment, 215, 216.
is the Junior Past Master, 211.
Jewel of, 211.
not an Officer, 211, 215.
position of, 211.
Initiation Ceremony, 106, 107, 132, 133, 134, 135, 136, 137, 153, 154, 199, 200, 206, 207, 242, 243.
Inman, H. F., 33.
Inner Guard(s), 77, 91, 93, 96, 97, 98, 99, 100, 101, 102, 103, 104, 105, 106, 107, 108, 109, 110, 111, 118, 130, 143, 154, 199, 200, 285, 286.
  Chair, 98.
  Jewel of, 96.
Innocence, Symbol of, 205.
Innovations, 136, 148, 149, 249.
'In Passing,' 78, 146, 172, 246.
Installation Addresses, 246.
Installation, Ceremony of, 170, 171, 172, 245, 246.
  Refreshment at irregular, 276.
  settled in 1827, 27.
Instruction, The Lodge of, 255, 256, 257, 258, 259, 260, 261, 262, 263, 264, 265, 266, 267, 268.
Intervals between Degrees, 230.
Intoxicating liquor during Installation, 276.

Jenks, J. H., 32, 51.
Jennings, Richard, 156.
Jewels, permissible, 161.
Joining other Degrees, 278.

Junior Deacon(s), 74, 107, 120, 127, 128, 129, 130, 131, 132, 133, 134, 135, 136, 137, 138, 139, 140, 141, 143, 145, 150, 153, 154, 163, 173, 200, 206, 207.
  Jewel of, 123, 142, 143.
  situation of, 130.
Junior Past Master, 211.
Junior Warden(s), 77, 91, 98, 100, 102, 103, 104, 105, 106, 107, 108, 109, 163, 187, 193, 198, 199, 200, 201, 202, 206, 248.
  Jewel of, 191, 198.
  position of column, 198.
  situation of, 198.
  when addressed by name, 100, 103, 233.

Kentish, W. G., 32.
Key, 184.
King, loyalty to the, 271.
King, toast of the, 248, 271.
Knaggs, S. A., 32, 69, 70.
Kneeling Stool, 100, 132, 138, 139, 140, 145, 150, 154.
Kneeling Stools, bulky, 138.
'Knife and fork' Masons, 280.
Knocks, 89, 90, 285, 286.
  for Candidates, 90, 91, 285, 286.
  muffled, 285, 286.
  on cuff, 285, 286.
  single, 90, 91.
  Table of, 285, 286.
  three distinct, 90.
  with left hand, 236, 237.

Lambskin, 205.
Lander, R. E. F., 32.
Landmarks, 192, 231.
Larkworthy, S. P., 34.
Late arrivals, 166.

Lectures, Emulation, 53, 54, 55, 56, 57, 58, 59.

Lectures, quotations from, 15, 87, 90, 131.

Lectures at Lodges of Instruction, 266, 267.

Lecture-Masters, 58, 59.

Left hand, knocks with, 236, 237.

    use of, by W.M., 236, 237, 242, 243, 244.

    wand transferred to, 127, 132, 133, 139, 140, 141, 145, 148, 150, 151, 154.

Letchworth, Sir Edward, 33, 35, 51, 287.

Letter 'G,' 201, 285, 286.

Level, 87, 191, 210.

Light, restoration to, 116, 134, 200, 206, 207, 242.

Lights, extinguishing of, 140, 145.

Lights, restoration of, 79, 148.

Lodge Committee, Incorrect description of, 277.

Lodge of Freemasons, 15.

Lodge ruled by Master and Wardens, 192.

Lodges of Instruction, 15, 27, 94, 126, 241, 255, 256, 257, 258, 259, 260, 261, 262, 263, 264, 265, 266, 267, 268, 280, 283, 284.

    announcement of Ceremony at, 262.

    Attendance Fees, 265.

    By-Laws, 265.

    election of Master, 260, 261.

    non-subscribing Members, 264, 265.

    smoking at, 264.

    the Lectures at, 266, 267.

Logic-working, 24.

London Rank, 162, 165, 173, 215, 278.

Lounge suits, 280.

Lyre, 114.

MACKEY, Dr A. G., 192.

McLaren, J. Russell, 52.

'Making' room, 54.

Masonic charms, 279.

Masonic clothing, 161, 173.

Masonic 'Don'ts,' 275, 276, 277, 278, 279, 280, 281.

Masonic expenditure, 278.

Masonry, teaching by catechism, 53, 54, 57.

Master(s), announcing ballots, 229.

    Collar not to be worn when visiting, 275.

    death of, 204, 212.

    duty to instal successor, 224, 225.

    election of, 218, 248.

    general hints for (during Labour), 246, 247, 248.

    general hints for (during Refreshment), 248, 249, 250, 251.

    has casting vote, 220.

    has custody of Warrant, 227.

    has no power to remove Officers, 224.

    may not act more than two years, 218.

    may not rule over more than one Lodge, 218.

    must not surrender Collar, 226.

    obligation, 217, 218.

    presides at all meetings, 219, 220.

    responsibilities, 227, 228, 229, 230, 231.

    responsible for ballots, 228, 229.

Master(s), returning salutes, 79.
  right to appoint Officers, 223, 224.
  right to conduct Ceremonies, 225, 226.
  right to decide work, 220.
  right to refuse admission, 221.
  right to rule, 219.
  ruling supreme, 220.
  work of, 233, 234, 235, 236, 237, 238, 239, 240, 241, 242, 243, 244, 245, 246.
Master-Elect, 170, 176, 245.
Match-box, The Emulation, 60, 61, 62, 63, 64, 281.
Meeting, days of, 198.
Middle Chamber, 80.
Minute Book, 127, 129, 178.
Minutes, 178, 181, 247.
Minutes, confirmation of, 179, 218, 219, 247.
Minutes, Grand Lodge, 25, 88.
Minutes at Lodge of Instruction, 255, 260.
Modern innovations, 136, 148, 149, 249.
' Moderns,' Grand Lodge of, 25, 29.
Monies of the Lodge, 185.
Morning dress, 161, 280.
Muffled knocks, 285, 286.
Murton, C. A., 32.
Music not essential, 114.
Music, secular, 116.
Musical programme, 248, 250.

NATIONAL ANTHEM, 250.
Naylor, Sir G., 156.
Neal, G. B. K., 97.
Nicholl, C. R. I., 156, 174.

Noisy behaviour at banquet, 195, 279.
Non-confirmation of Minutes, 179, 180, 219.
North-East corner, correct position at, 135.
North London working, 24.

OBLIGATION, Correct Sns. for, 79, 80, 133, 139, 141, 147, 148, 151, 154, 242, 243, 244.
Obligation, First Degree, 133, 154, 242.
Obligation, Second Degree, 139, 151, 243.
Obligation, Third Degree, 141, 147, 148, 244.
Officers of the Lodge, 85, 86.
Officers, permanent, 119, 158.
Officers, permissive, 85, 86, 111, 155, 187.
Offices, declaring vacant, 171, 245.
Offices, progressive, 111, 112, 118, 120.
Officials, permanent, 119, 158, 177.
Oliver, Dr, 192.
Opening in the Second Degree, 103, 104, 235.
Opening in the Third Degree, 104, 235, 236.
Opening Ode, 115, 233.
Opening the Lodge, 103, 233, 234, 235.
Oratory, how to improve, 194.
Orde, G. P., 34.
Organist, 114, 115, 116, 117, 119, 250.
Organist, Jewel of, 114.
Oxford-working, 24.

PASSING, Ceremony of, 107, 108, 137, 138, 139, 150, 151, 152, 153, 200, 201, 208, 209, 243.
Passing the port-decanter, 75.
Past Master's Jewel, 211.
Peace and Knowledge, Symbol of, 123.
'Peculiar system of morality,' 73.
Perfect Ceremonies of Craft Masonry, 18.
Perfection of Ritual, 280.
Permanent Officers, 119, 158.
Permanent Officials, 119, 158, 177.
Permissible Jewels, 161.
Permissive Officers, 85, 86, 111, 155, 187.
Perseverance, United Lodge of, 27, 28, 29, 56, 57.
Peter Gilkes. *See under Gilkes.*
Peyton, A. J., 33, 71, 72.
Pike, James, 32.
Plenty, emblem of, 95.
Plumb Rule, 191, 198, 202.
Poniard, 101, 102, 106, 154.
Poniard, method for I.G. to apply, 101.
Precepting, 257, 258, 259, 266, 267, 268.
Preceptor(s), 15, 280.
  powers of, 257.
  qualifications of, 257, 258.
  teaching should be individual, 267, 268.
  word should be law, 257.
Preferment among Masons, 14, 15.
Preston, William, 55, 56.
Preston's Lectures, 55, 56.
'Principal Officers upstanding,' 196.

Printed Rituals, 18, 23, 125, 126.
Processional entry into the Lodge, 162, 163, 164.
Processional retirement from the Lodge, 172, 173, 215.
'Profit and Pleasure,' 122, 189, 281.
Pro Grand Master, visit by, 246.
Progress, no Brother can claim, 111, 112, 193.
Progressive Office, 111, 112, 118, 120.
Promotion, methods of, 14.
Prompting by Deacons, 126.
Prompting in the Lodge, 169, 213.
Promulgation, Lodge of, 29, 30, 53, 123.
Proposal forms, 230.
Proposing Candidates, need for caution, 276.
'Prove the Lodge close-tyled,' 104, 105.
Provincial Assistant Grand Master, visit by, 246.
Provincial Deputy Grand Master, visit by, 246.
Provincial Grand Master, visit by, 246.
Provincial Grand Rank, 162, 165, 167, 173, 215, 278.
'Proving' visitors, 170, 199.
Public Nights of Grand Stewards' Lodge, 38, 39, 40, 41, 42, 43, 44, 45, 46, 47, 48, 49, 50, 51, 52.

QUORUM in Lodge, 230.

RAISING, Ceremony of, 108, 109, 139, 140, 141, 144, 145, 146, 147, 148, 149, 150, 201, 202, 209, 210, 244.

Rankin, G. J. V., 32, 66, 67, 68.

Recognised Lodges of Instruction, 283, 284.

Reconciliation, Lodge of, 24, 26, 27, 28, 29, 30, 40, 41, 43, 44, 51, 57, 287.

Reconciliation ritual, 24, 27, 28, 31, 38, 41, 42, 43, 51, 287.

Record, accuracy of, 179, 180, 219.

' Recovering,' 104, 108, 141, 202, 209, 210, 236, 244, 275, 276.

Red Apron Lodges, 37.

Refreshment, 95, 117, 173, 177, 194, 195, 196, 215, 216, 248, 249, 250, 251, 279.

at Lodges of Instruction, 263, 264.

seating at, 173, 174.

smoking at, 248, 249, 269, 270, 271, 272, 273, 274.

Regular Officers of the Lodge, 85, 86.

Removal of Officers, 224.

' Report ' v. ' Alarm,' 90.

Reports, Inner Guard's, 98, 99, 102, 105, 106, 107, 108, 109.

Junior Warden's, 199, 200, 201.

Restoration of Lights, 79, 148.

Restoration to Light, 116, 134, 200, 206, 207, 242.

Restraint, symbol of, 95.

Resuming the Lodge, 241.

Richards, A. A., 32, 51.

Richardson, Frank, 156.

Risings, business for the, 237, 238, 239.

Ritual not binding, 90.

Ritualists, expert, 280.

Rituals, printed, 18, 23, 125, 126.

Robbins, Sir Alfred, 157.

Roberts, J. F., 63.

Rucker, J. A., 51.

Rushton, F. T., 32, 51.

Russell, J., 51.

SACRIFICE of decorum, 129.

Sadler, H., 25, 28, 42.

' Salutes ' v. ' Greetings,' 168, 169.

Salutes to Grand Officers, 166, 167.

' Saving Time,' 129, 136, 148, 153.

Scott, A., 32, 51.

Seating of Brethren in Lodge, 165.

Second Tracing Board, 139, 153, 201, 209, 243.

Secretary, 74, 89, 92, 94, 95, 99, 111, 112, 113, 119, 163, 176, 177, 178, 179, 180, 181, 182, 183, 184, 185, 186, 192, 230.

exempt from subscription, 181, 182.

Jewel of, 176.

should be a P.M., 177.

Secrets, position for communicating, 79, 146.

Secular music, 116.

' See that the Lodge is properly tyled,' 103, 104.

' Seek and ye shall find,' 90.

Senior Deacon, 101, 108, 109, 127, 128, 129, 132, 138, 139, 140, 141, 142, 143, 144, 145, 146, 147, 148, 149, 150, 151, 152, 153, 154, 163, 173, 192, 208, 209.

Jewel of, 123, 142, 143.

situation of, 142.

Senior Warden, 54, 77, 78, 92, 101, 130, 133, 135, 140, 141, 151, 152, 163, 191, 192, 193, 204, 205, 206, 207, 208, 209, 210.
Jewel of, 191.
position of column, 204.
rules Lodge in Master's absence, 204, 205.
when addressed by name, 233.
Seniority of Deacons reversed, 132, 153.
Serving Brother, 87.
Sheet should never be folded, 79, 140, 145.
'Showing off,' 226.
Sick Brethren, visiting of, 189.
'Side' Degrees, 278.
Sign during Obs., 79, 80, 133, 139, 141, 147, 148, 151, 154, 242, 243, 244.
Sign of R. *v.* Sign of F., 275.
Signs, when to use, 76, 77, 78.
Silent salutes, 168, 169.
Simmonds, Frank W., 34.
'Sir,' Worshipful, 279.
Smith, Gordon, 50.
Smith, Sir Colville, 34, 35.
Smoking at Refreshment, 248, 249, 269, 270, 271, 272, 273, 274.
in Lodges of Instruction, 264.
when permissible, 248, 249, 269, 270, 271, 272, 273, 274.
Social board, 195.
Sorbet, 248, 249, 271, 272, 273, 274.
South-East corner, correct position at, 153.
Spaull, F. R., 32.

Speaking, how to improve, 194.
Speed, emblem of, 142.
Square, 87, 101, 102, 108, 139, 161, 214, 235.
method for Inner Guard to apply, 101.
Squares, levels, and perpendiculars, 275.
Squaring the Lodge, 73, 74, 75, 133, 134, 140, 145, 150, 152, 153.
Stability Lodge of Instruction, 57.
Step, the, 98, 100, 103, 104, 105, 106, 107, 108, 128, 133, 134, 139, 145, 148, 149, 150, 151, 152, 154, 199, 200, 201, 202, 206, 207, 208, 209, 210, 242, 243, 244, 245, 276.
Steward, 93, 94, 95.
Steward, a useful Officer, 94.
Steward, Jewel of, 95.
Steward, Junior, 93.
Steward, Senior, 93.
Steward, Wine, 93.
Subscription, Secretary exempt from, 181, 182.
Substituted secrets of a M.M., 236.
Sudlow, R. C., 32, 34, 35, 48, 62, 288.
Summons, 183, 220, 247.
Sussex, Duke of, 26, 46.
Symbolism of squaring, 73, 74, 75.

Table of Knocks, 285, 286.
'Taking Wine,' 215, 216, 249.
Tasker, H. C., 33, 72.
Three Grand Principles, 186, 281.
Three Great Lights, 89, 188.

Time-table, 248.

Toasts, should Wardens stand for ?, 195, 196.

Tracing Boards, changing, 127, 129, 171.
  changing during Installation, 171.
  second, 139, 153, 201, 209, 243.

Treasurer, 88, 94, 95, 112, 119, 158, 163, 181, 184, 185, 186, 187, 192, 248, 278.
  Jewel of, 184.

Trowel, 96.

Turning movements, 128.

Tyler, insuring the, 182.

Tyler(s), 87, 88, 89, 90, 91, 92, 98, 99, 102, 103, 104, 105, 106, 107, 108, 109, 110, 112, 158, 161, 172, 234, 248, 278.

Tyler's toast, 87.

Udall, J., 51.

Undress regalia incorrect at Installations, 278.

Union, Articles of, 26.

Union, the, 25.

United Lodge of Perseverance, 27, 28, 29, 56, 57.

Universal-working, 24.

Vacant, declaring Offices, 171, 245.

Visiting sick Brethren, 189.

Visitors and the Charity Box, 117, 118.

Visitors entering after the Lodge is open, 165.

Visitors from Foreign Constitutions, 166.

Visitors, proving unknown, 170, 199.

V.S.L., 129, 134, 172, 187, 214, 234, 235.
  correct position of, 214, 235.

Wand(s), Deacons', 127, 129, 132, 133, 135, 139, 140, 141, 145, 148, 150, 151, 154, 163.
  D.C.'s, 170.
  when Deacons need not carry, 127.

Warden(s), 191, 192, 193, 194, 195, 196, 197, 202, 209.
  chair, 94, 95.
  responsibilities during Refreshment, 195, 196.
  standing for toasts, 195, 196.
  use of gavel by, 195.
  See also under 'Junior Warden' and 'Senior Warden.'

Warrant, 227, 246.
  Master responsible for, 227.

Webster, Sir Augustus, 62.

West End working, 24.

White, W. H., 29, 41, 42, 43, 44, 47, 51.

White gloves, 161.

White ties, 280.

White waistcoats, 280.

Wilson, A. B., 33, 70, 71.

Wilson, S. B., 30, 31, 32, 44, 45, 46.

'Wine' Steward, 93.

Wisdom, Symbol of, 142.

'Without detriment,' 278.

Woods, Sir A., 156.

Woods, Sir William, 156.

Word-perfection of Ritual, 280.

Working Tools, explanation of, 243, 246.

Worshipful Master. See under Master.

Printed by Neill & Co., Ltd., Edinburgh.

Lightning Source UK Ltd.
Milton Keynes UK
UKOW022044281012

201323UK00009B/13/P